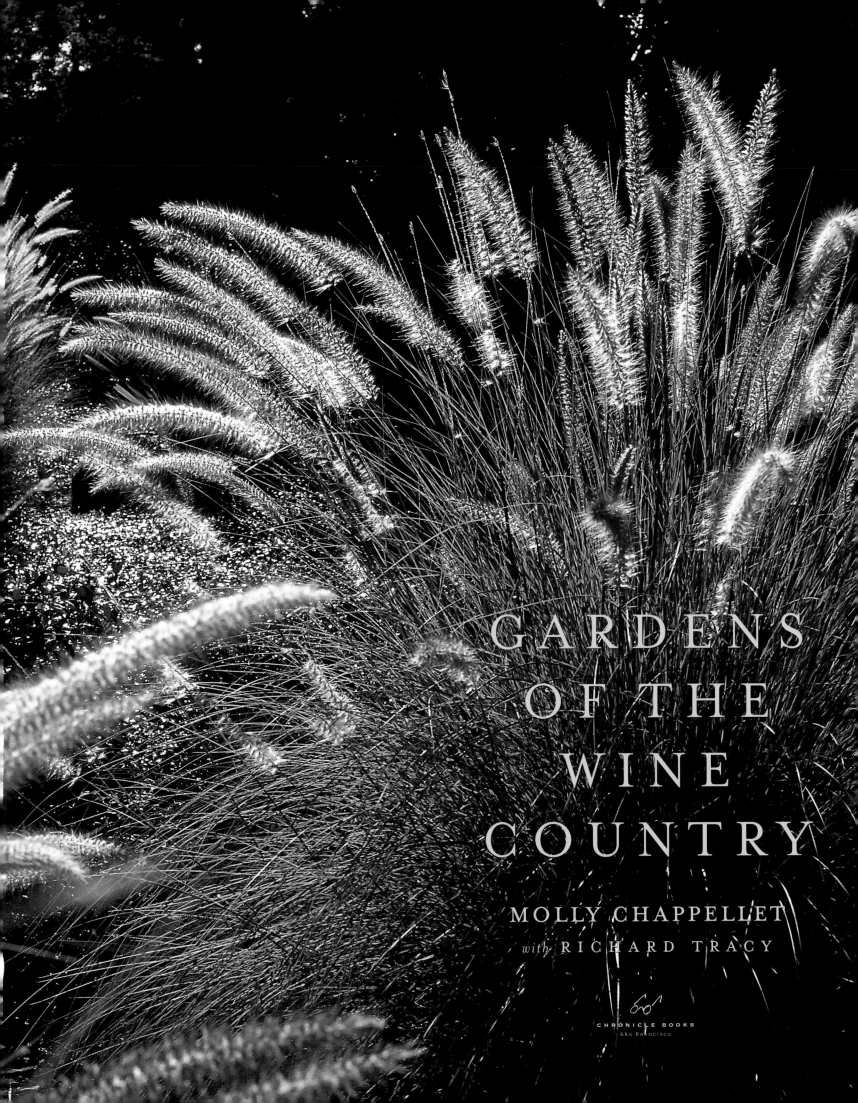

GARDENS
OF THE
WINE
COUNTRY

MOLLY CHAPPELLET

with RICHARD TRACY

CHRONICLE BOOKS
SAN FRANCISCO

DEDICATION

IN MEMORY OF MY MOTHER, CATHERINE, WHO COULD
MAKE ANYTHING GROW,
AND MY FATHER, JOHN, WHO NOURISHED ALL.

M.C.

FOR FELICIA, FOR CONTINUING LOVING SUPPORT
OF A LONG-TERM PROJECT.

R.T.

❊ Library of Congress Cataloging-in-Publication Data: Chappellet, Molly. Gardens of the wine country/by Molly Chappellet with Richard Tracy. p. cm. ❊ ISBN 0-8118-1697-4 (hc) ❊ 1. Gardens—California—Napa Valley. 2. Gardens—California—Napa Valley—Pictorial works. I. Tracy, Richard. II. Title. ❊ SB466.U65N363 1998 ❊ 712'.6'0979419—dc21 ❊ 97-52215 ❊ CIP ❊ Manufactured in China ❊ Designed by Aufuldish & Warinner ❊ Distributed in Canada by Raincoast Books: 9050 Shaughnessy Street, Vancouver, British Columbia V6P 6E5 ❊

10 9 8 7 6 5 4   ❊ Chronicle Books: 85 Second Street, San Francisco, California 94105 ❊ Web Site: www.chroniclebooks.com

INTRODUCTION

I F you were to float silently over the length of California's famed Napa Valley in a hot air balloon, you would be enthralled with the sight of lush vineyards, wineries, and magnificent gardens that, on the ground, would be tucked out of sight. I have been fortunate to see these gardens from the air and from the ground, because this valley is my home. I feel very privileged to be allowed to share with you these magnificent private gardens of my friends in the Napa Valley.

During the past thirty years, I have been in most of these gardens many times. Often I've come just to enjoy the garden with a friend. Other times I have seen them as backdrops to parties; sometimes I have helped make them part of a special occasion—a wedding, a debutante party, or an anniversary. I've come to know the gardens well. I've even dug in them, pruned or fed plants to encourage perfect timing of blooms, added or moved plants. Although the owners live very involved and different lives, they all have one thing in common: they love, love, love their gardens, whether they work in them, supervise those who do, or simply enjoy them on weekends.

It is amazing how, even though there may be a designer involved in the organization of the garden, the owner's personality usually speaks out—"Show me the garden, I'll show you the person." You will have the opportunity to know these extraordinary people through their *extra*ordinary gardens.

Something unexpected happened to me while researching this book. I fell in love with each garden over and over again. I found that looking at these gardens through the lens of a camera gave me a fresh appreciation of the design, as well as the plant combinations and forms, in each one. When I was alone and took a little time in these places, they began to speak to me in their own languages. No matter how similar the plant material and design might appear, each garden had its own rhythm and personality—its own music. Some echoed the free flow of jazz, others brought operatic arias to mind.

While each of these gardens plays a distinctly different theme, continuity is derived not only from the climate but from the scenic backdrop of the vineyards. Napa Valley's giant vineyard garden is well maintained—green all summer, golden and amber in the fall, sculptural and haunting in the winter, and brought back to life against soft billows of mustard in the springtime.

The climate here allows us to grow almost anything. Temperature variations give us the beautiful change of seasons without the disadvantage of long, burdensome winters. How thrilled I was when we moved from Southern California to find I could have peonies, tulips, and lilacs galore, which all love the cold days and nights of our winters. In addition to the things that love the cold, we can grow palm trees, citrus, and bougainvillea, if we are willing to protect them.

Now before all you garden-lovers start packing your bags, I should tell you that we gardeners here in the Napa Valley have our own set of challenges. We struggle all summer long to maintain our gardens. With precious little rain

PAGE 3: *Peter Newton's rose arbor. Be they small or large, formal or wild, these gardens of the Napa Valley all adjoin vineyards. Vistas of the immaculate rows of vines either hide between the plantings or are featured in a Versailles-like panorama.* ABOVE *is a hillside of Chappellet Vineyard;* OPPOSITE, FROM TOP TO BOTTOM, *are Peter Newton's weeping cherry trees in circular box hedges, Lukie Chappellet peering out from the vegetable garden, and Annie Fisher's twin garden houses and her rose arbor.*

during that season and temperatures that can hover around 100 degrees for days, many plants are miserable. One dares not leave a beloved garden in the summer, lest it up and die.

What most visitors do not realize is that the Napa Valley is really a spring and fall garden region. We have an early false spring in February, when the almond trees burst forth and the mustard blooms between the dark trunks of the bare grapevines. Then more cold weather sets in before the real spring of late March and April. Pink and white blossoming apples, peaches, plums, purple lilac, long sprays of delicate white spirea and narcissus, daffodils, tulips, and hundreds of other flowering plants bloom in harmony and profusion. Equally magnificent is the colorful fall. There is a horizontal glow to the Valley from the copper, gold, and amber vines with the accenting of golden oaks and maples on the surrounding hills.

Both seasons go too quickly, leaving those long, hot summers—which are exactly what the grapevines need. Relief, however, from the summer heat comes from coastal fog, which flows up over the Mayacamas Mountains from the west. It adds moisture to both gardens and vineyards, helping to produce the premium wines for which the Valley is famous.

Gardeners everywhere—from the Napa Valley to New Jersey to New Zealand— no matter what the climatic or cultural differences, are kindred spirits. Although we may have little else in common, we are a family of people who love plants and want to share ideas about them—how to grow them, how to combine them in the most interesting ways, how to control problems. Most of all, we want to share our passions. Thus we have asked many of our gardeners here in the Napa Valley to share one or two specific suggestions that will be applicable wherever you live and garden. A collection of these "Tips from Our Gardeners" is included at the end of the book.

My collaborator on this book, Richard Tracy, is the well-known *Sacramento Bee* garden editor. We have known each other for many years and have been talking about doing this project for some time. Not only has it been fun working with Dick, but it has been interesting to see what things drew his attention. We believe the combination of my artistic background and Dick's journalistic one, plus the differences in our male/female responses, have added a richer dimension to this work. Thanks to Dick's gentle but probing questions, you will have the advantage of hearing the gardener's voice. I have added personal observations about my friends and about the gardens as I have known them.

Dick and I visited each of the gardens in this book several times. Sometimes we came calling at less-than-convenient times; first light and dinnertime were our favorite hours. We are enormously grateful to the owners for producing these works of beauty and poetry, and for allowing us all to enter their very private worlds. ❧

HERE IN CALIFORNIA, ANYTHING OVER A HUNDRED YEARS OLD IS OLD. AFTER ALL, WE WERE NOT EVEN A PART OF THE UNITED STATES UNTIL THE MID-NINETEENTH CENTURY. MANY OF OUR TREES HAVE SEEN QUITE A FEW CENTURIES PASS BY, BUT AS FAR AS OUR GARDENS ARE CONCERNED, WE ARE CERTAINLY INFANTS, ESPECIALLY WHEN YOU CONSIDER THAT THE CHINESE AND EGYPTIANS WERE LANDSCAPING THREE THOUSAND TO FOUR THOUSAND YEARS AGO! ✳ THE INTRODUCTION OF GARDENS TO THE NAPA VALLEY PARALLELED THE FIRST PLANTINGS OF VINEYARDS—AROUND 1860— WHEN HORSE-DRAWN BUCKBOARDS WERE THE ONLY MEANS OF TRANSPORTATION, AND CLEARING THE LAND WAS DONE BY HAND AND HORSE. AND YET THE HERITAGE OF THESE EARLY GARDENS IS EVEN OLDER THAN THEIR STRUCTURE. THEIR CREATORS BROUGHT WITH THEM THE LEGACIES AND FORMS OF EUROPEAN HOMELANDS AND, IN THESE VENERABLE LANDSCAPES, PROVIDED THE FOUNDATION OF WHAT HAS MADE THE NAPA VALLEY A SYMBOL OF OLD WORLD CHARM.

OLD
GARDENS

✳

ECHOES OF THE PAST

SOME OF THE GARDENS IN THE NAPA VALLEY CLEARLY REVEAL THEIR

EUROPEAN ROOTS. AROUND THE TURN OF THE CENTURY, MOST OF

THE PEOPLE WHO SETTLED HERE CAME FROM FRANCE, ITALY, OR

GERMANY. THE SULLIVANS' GARDEN AT BEAULIEU ILLUSTRATES BOTH

A FRENCH AND AN ITALIAN INFLUENCE. GERMAN HERITAGE CAN BE

SEEN AT SCHRAMSBERG AND KRUG. AN ENGLISH CONNECTION CAN

BE FELT IN MANY OF THE VICTORIAN HOMES AND GARDENS—SUCH AS

THE ONES AT SPOTTSWOODE, THE HILLSES', AND THE COPPOLAS'.

THE GARDENS OF BEAULIEU BEGIN THIS BOOK FOR MANY reasons. They were the first gardens I visited when we moved to the Napa Valley in the late sixties. But even more important, and why Beaulieu makes a great starting place to view the gardens of the wine country, is Beaulieu's heritage. The gardens are a Californian evocation of classic French and Italian landscapes. In much the same way that the wines of the Napa Valley honor European winemaking traditions while creating a distinctive magic that is entirely their own, the gardens of Beaulieu are a New World rendition of Old World gardening styles.

"My grandparents, Monsieur and Madame de Latour, bought the property in 1900 and named it *Beaulieu*—French for 'beautiful place,'" Dagmar Sullivan explains. "Of course, when they first arrived, all that was here were hay fields and oaks!" At that time the property was 125 acres, and most of the acreage was eventually planted to grapes. The vineyards, along with the name of the winery, were sold to liquor conglomerate Heublein in 1969.

"It was my American-born grandmother who laid out the formal Italian garden and the pleached sycamores in the 1930s," Dagmar says. "Over the years the garden had been let go and we had to do a great deal to restore it. We couldn't have done it without the help of our head gardener Antonio Gallegos. He has worked with us for twenty-eight years and has been wonderful."

The first impression of Beaulieu begins at Highway 29, with a handsome dark green metal gate and a long, long avenue of unpruned plane trees. Behind the trees, manicured vineyards line both sides of the drive. From this entrance, you arrive at a neatly raked courtyard, where you must decide whether to park or continue over the bridge down the drive to the house. The grandeur of the garden, with its gigantic ancient oaks, elms, and maples, and the formality of the sunken terrace make the good-size house appear small and almost insignificant. Only the California-style architecture and low white rail fence reveal that this garden is not in Italy.

Adults might see this garden as quiet and formal, but children get excited about following the many trails. The paths at Beaulieu are an invitation to the unknown. They offer a sense of discovery that both adults and children find irresistible. At the end of the paths are glimpses of a few of the garden's treasures: fountains bubbling inside a ring of cypress trees or a handsome black barn. But most of the

PREVIOUS PAGES: *Pond at Coppolas, fountain court at Spottswoode.* OPPOSITE AND RIGHT: *The formal garden at Beaulieu Vineyards, framed by dark sentries of Italian cypress, reflects the French and Italian heritage of the valley. Mme. de Latour laid out the garden in the 1930s. The dream-like setting, with its classical statuary, massive ancient oaks, and vineyards is the stage for many outdoor celebrations.*

PREVIOUS PAGES: *Gigantic valley oaks* (Quercus lobata), *camellias, and box hedges surround Beaulieu's main lawn area, creating a splendid shaded park. The maturity of the oaks and shrubs lends credence to its claim as the most venerable of Napa Valley gardens. The pollarded plane trees, shown here in leaf and during winter, took thirty years to form their canopy of branches.*

paths need to be followed to divulge their secrets, such as the rose-hung tennis court, the vegetable garden, the greenhouses, the rose garden, and the sunken Italian garden with its central, rectangular pond.

Maintaining gardens this extensive and ambitious is becoming more and more of a challenge. The Sullivans have wisely addressed this problem by regularly renting out their facilities to selected groups.

As Dick and I came to this garden to photograph, nearly thirty years after my first visit, my overriding feeling was one of serenity and harmony, rather than grandeur. Beaulieu is the kind of place where one longs to spend more time—to stroll down the broad, shaded walkways created by years of rigorous pruning and trellising of the sycamores. The paths are all the more inviting, having been narrowed by dense growth of vines and roses, and the stream bed has become neatly edged with a rich blanket of *Vinca major* hugging the banks on both sides.

The many different sections of the garden are united in a graceful flow from one area to another, often stitched together by wide graveled paths, with hedges and trees helping to define the spaces. The powerful presence of an enormous four-hundred-year-old oak tree also underlines the strength of this garden, which is its original, well thought out, beautifully proportioned plan. Dagmar Sullivan has carefully maintained the initial concept while improving the appearance of the grand old estate with her meticulous care and wise selections of plants. Fortunately, she has not allowed bright or exotic planting that would distract from the quiet, park-like theme of ancient trees, lawn, and shrubs. Other than the roses in the rose garden, all the plants are white: star jasmine around the house, masses of white agapanthus, white petunias in pots, and white begonias which line the path from the bridge to the front lawn.

Acknowledging that Beaulieu is most likely the oldest Napa Valley estate to have remained in the same family, Dagmar observes, "It's the garden that makes the property what it is. The houses are very simple. We enjoy that simplicity and while we're alive they will stay that way."

Standing at attention, sycamores line the drive, welcoming visitors to Beaulieu Vineyards. There is a serenity and harmony to this garden that balance its grandeur. BELOW: *Majestic oaks and a Deodar cedar thrive along a creek which courses through the garden.*

IF IT'S FEBRUARY OR EARLY MARCH AND YOU'RE DRIVING north on the main highway through the Napa Valley—the one that dips under the arch of elm trees just beyond St. Helena—your eye will be pulled immediately to the right by a brilliant field of mustard with rows of dark, dormant vines leading up to billowy pink blossoms and the German-style roof line of the Charles Krug winery. Though spring is officially a few weeks away, this field seems to promise everything good in the season.

Following the road to the winery, you come close enough to the flowering fruit trees to notice that there are blossoms of many different colors on a single tree. It was just such a springtime drive that introduced me to Blanche Mondavi's lovely garden.

March and April are the most exciting months to be here. Early on, it's the Chinese magnolias that sing out against their bare branches while the rest of the garden is still asleep. Then come the flowering plum and peach trees in shades of white to deep pink. The two-story camellia bushes start to bring the nearby house alive, color-drenched blooms against dark, glossy leaves. But the climax takes place when the giant azaleas, followed by the rhododendrons, burst in full glory. The good-looking, two-story main residence—a dark brown, shingled redwood—disappears as a shadow behind light pink camellias, white azaleas, deep pink rhododendrons, and hanging clusters of lavender wisteria.

When Blanche and Peter Mondavi moved back to the family home in 1978 after Peter's mother, Rosa Mondavi, died, they began clearing out some of the overgrown areas and increasing the lawn perimeter, creating an even greater park-like effect. Much of this garden can be viewed simply by standing in one place and slowly making a 360-degree turn.

Blanche says, "I love this old-fashioned garden and home, and I've only tried to simplify it. Of course I couldn't help adding a lot of white 'Alaska' azaleas and hundreds of roses."

The 1914 house, designed by Willis Polk, a prominent San Francisco architect, is still a youngster compared to the 250-year-old oaks or the 100-year-old *Rosa banksiae* climbing one of the majestic trunks. In this old, comfortable, and charming setting, the ancient trees—some of which were brought by railroad since there were no nurseries—have witnessed great moments of winemaking history.

It's reassuring to know that the sons of Blanche and Peter Mondavi, who also live on the property, are not only carrying on the great Krug winemaking tradition, but are enjoying adding beauty to the grounds as well. So as the years go by, the many different varieties of oaks will continue to record Krug history. ❦

The Willis Polk home is haloed in fragrance and beauty by its rambling wisteria vine, and skirted in color by azaleas and camellias. Three varieties of cherry grafted onto one tree at the entrance to the Charles Krug Winery and Blanche Mondavi's garden create a symphony in one movement.

OPPOSITE: A one-hundred-year-old Rosa banksiae *climbs a two-hundred-year-old oak.*

OPPOSITE: *The cupola of the winery is framed against blooming dogwoods and azaleas.* RIGHT: *From Highway 29, we see the spring show of mustard in bloom among slumbering grapevines at Charles Krug.* ABOVE: *Dogwoods thrive here in the Valley's cold winters. They catch our eye and lead it to flowering azaleas across the lawn as the homes of dark redwood disappear like shadows behind the flowering shrubs.*

ABOVE: *Reflecting a gentler era, the porch of Jack and Jamie Davies' home at historic Schramsberg is a watercolorist's delight with its potted ferns, 'King Alfred' daffodils, and 'Ile de France' tulips.* RIGHT: *The couple's sense of humor is reflected in the fish pond's exuberant bronze frog statue, "Riddler's Night Out."* OPPOSITE: *A carriageway of stately Mission olives leads to the vineyard.*

IT HAD BEEN YEARS SINCE I HAD VISITED THE DAVIES. WHEN Dick and I went to Schramsberg to photograph the garden, I was brought to tears. Thirty years ago, Jack and Jamie Davies were one of the first couples my husband and I met in the Napa Valley. (In fact, Jack stored our first vintage—1968—in his caves, since we had not yet completed our winery.)

I well remember the outline of paths and beds with old moss-covered rock borders. Nothing much planted anywhere—only beautiful old trees. To see what two people with determination, sensitivity, and an unbelievable amount of work have done at Schramsberg was overwhelming. The Davies have restored the history of the place inside and out. It was not done in one fell swoop; it has taken years—one section at a time—to reclaim the original intent and create the beauty one now sees.

"Our gardens are an extension of nature," explains Jamie, "and we tried to work them into the framework of the olive, redwood, and eucalyptus trees that existed here as nature's backdrop." They felt it was important to preserve the surroundings as well as the property's ancient hand-dug caves, which have been declared a state historical landmark.

"Actually, I feel that the garden begins at the foot of the driveway," Jamie says. Robert Louis Stevenson described it in *The Silverado Squatters*: "A rude trail rapidly mounting; a little stream . . . big enough perhaps after the rains, but already yielding up its life; overhead and

on all sides a bower of green and tangled thicket, still fragrant . . . with thimble-berry . . . and the buckeyes were putting forth their twisted horns of blossom; through all this, we struggled toughly upwards, canted to and fro by the roughness of the trail." And although the road is smooth now, the ambience is much as it was when Stevenson and his wife, Fanny, honeymooned at the Schram estate.

Narrow footpaths still wander about between the planting beds edged with low volcanic rock walls. "We have very shallow soil here," Jamie observes, "and without the container beds the rains would wash everything away. Besides, the irregularity of the rock seems to soften the harsh lines of the buildings and the parking lot."

For those who venture beyond the parking area, one road to the vineyards is lined with a long avenue of century-old sculptural olives, which were planted strictly for their beauty in the 1870s. Off to one side is a truly magical picnic area beneath a ring of towering redwoods. Streaks of sunlight penetrating here and there between the branches echo the spiritual environment of a cathedral. Fed by an underground aquifer, the giant redwoods thrive even during periods of prolonged drought.

With natural and man-made elements combined, the landscape fulfills the needs of the Davies: "The garden is an extension of the life we enjoy here," Jamie concludes, "and it's an integral part of being a grower and producer of wines." ❦

RIGHT: *Tucked along the edge of Schramsberg's visitor parking area, the herb, cutting, and bulb garden is a standout in spring. This is one of a few gardens where Jamie allows bright color. In the rest of the landscape, there are no formal plantings or harsh colors to detract from its natural charm.* OPPOSITE: *Curving through towering redwoods, the driveway prepares visitors for the sight of the majestic four-story Victorian. One wonders if a similar sense of awe was felt by Robert Louis Stevenson when he was a house guest of the original owners almost 110 years ago.* OPPOSITE BOTTOM: *The entrance to Schramberg's caves, hand-dug by Chinese workmen in 1870, now a California historical landmark.*

WHEN YOU DRIVE THROUGH THE ARCHED GATES OF Spottswoode, you feel as if you've come home. There's a warm familiarity, a sense of nostalgia. The vine-covered pillars, the old-fashioned azalea and camellia bushes, the charming Victorian home, and the graceful drive around the big green lawn supporting ancient oaks and hundred-foot palms all welcome you. This romantic garden typifies the Victorian gardens of the nineteenth century, with winding paths and small, irregular flower beds edged in fieldstone, like the ones at Schramsberg.

Mary Novak, owner of Spottswoode, is a gardener's gardener; it is absolutely impossible for her to pass a weed without pulling it, no matter whose garden it's in. For as long as she can remember, Mary has been interested in gardening. "I was always potting things up," she recalls. "When I was a small child I had so many plants that my father built me a lath house."

"Gardening is a learning process," she professes. "I used to think if you put something in the ground, you were stuck with it forever. Now I just say, 'Nah, I don't like that!' But I have a hard time taking out a plant to throw it away because they're like friends. So I generally try to move them somewhere else.

"When we first moved in though," she continues, "I decided not to rip out anything at all for a full year, so we could see for sure what we had here—what special surprises there might be. That turned out to be a great lesson, and the big reward was magnificent peonies. I hadn't known about them in our Southern California gardens."

Besides Mary's constant devotion, it's the enormous old trees that make this garden remarkable. Notable specimens include the Japanese pagoda tree, the magnolias (including a *Magnolia denudata* with totally white blossoms), an Italian cypress, a bay tree, and a locust, complemented by the valley oaks (*Quercus lobata*) growing in the front lawn.

The pathways that wind among the planting beds and trees in the garden are part of the original design. Alongside the house is a circular bed where Mary delights in trying out several new roses each year. The adjacent beds are devoted to annuals: "This is just about the only place I plant annuals," Mary acknowledges. "The rest of the grounds are in bulbs and perennials."

Pausing at the front steps to the expansive porch as the garden tour ends, Mary gazes lovingly at her home. "I don't know what will happen to this place after I'm gone. I'd like to leave it to a trust, so it could be preserved for its architecture and garden. It's a fun place to live. I love it, and look forward to spending the rest of my life here." ☙

ABOVE: *Varying shades of pink in the 'Apricot Beauty' tulip echo the color of the brick at poolside. The landscaped acres at Spottswoode include a tennis court, vegetable garden, ornamental gardens, and an arboretum in addition to the pool. Mary says this is "a family garden, not a showplace."*

OPPOSITE: *This lovely Japanese pagoda tree (Sophora japonica 'Pendula') has taken years to develop its gracefully contorted trunk.*

When Mary bought this lovely Victorian with its gracious veran-dah patterned after the Hotel del Coronado in San Diego, gardening was a family affair. The boys mowed the lawn and raked the driveway, while the girls worked with Mary in the flower and veg-etable beds. ABOVE: A lofty California fan palm (Washing-tonia filifera) catches a breeze in foliage 130 feet above the ground. LEFT: Cascading over the entrance gate is an old rambler, 'American Pillar', whose brilliant color and rigorous character more than make up for its lack of scent.

Reminiscent of many early California farmsteads, towering palms grace Erika Hills' front lawn with its circular driveway. A weeping willow, flowering cherry, and Lady Banks' rose bask in the sunlight of a spring morning.

"La Donna della Grapa," an

alpine stone statue from Florence,

reigns in a graceful pose, festooned

with grapes. Her veil of gold moss is

echoed in the golden Euonymus

shrubs. Encircled by peonies and

nearly engulfed by a climbing white

rose, this gazebo, left, provides

shade in the summer and a viewing

spot for afternoon tea at the edge of

the vineyard.

IT'S NOT THAT PALMS ARE STRANGERS TO NAPA VALLEY gardens—there is one at Beaulieu, there are more at Schramsberg and the Niebaum-Coppola estate, and of course, there's that very tall, skinny palm at Spottswoode. But at the Hillses', the whole tone of the garden is palms, all over a hundred years old, in splendid shape, waving in the afternoon breeze.

Trees, like people, have their own personalities—the soft, gentle pepper tree; the romantic weeping willow; the dignified, grand old oak; but there's a kind of tropical royalty to the palms. Unusually shaped for a tree, they are yet stately and friendly and represent a kind of exotica that evokes the Victorian period.

Erika, a former Austrian ski champion, now delights in her garden. She loves to entertain, and Austin, co-owner of Grgich Hills Winery, loves to cook. To keep fresh produce close at hand, Erika planted an extensive vegetable garden and fruit and nut trees. "We have fruits of one kind or another ten months of the year. First cherries, then early peaches, nectarines, plums—then more peaches, pears, and apples into fall along with hazelnuts and pistachios. Then very late in the year come the kiwis and, by January, the citrus.

"Of course I *love* flowers," she enthuses, an echo of Austrian Alps still coloring her voice. So she has planted roses, sweet-smelling vines, and a marvelous stand of hollyhocks against the house. Erika says we should come back in a year or two when the new plantings of roses have climbed the tall trunks of the palm trees. I can hardly wait.

Her palette of apricot, peach, and all shades of lavender can be found in floral patterns in the house as well as the garden. Flowers from her garden, besides supplying material for her large-scale arrangements, also provide inspiration for her painted furniture, which is sold in her St. Helena shop, Erika Hills—The Painted Illusion.

Erika chose the dramatic color of the 'Don Juan' rose in one corner of the garden because, she says, "everyone should have a Don Juan in her life. We all need that. Then I planted the 'Fantasy' grape, not just because it's the best eating grape, but because we all need fantasy, too.

"Don't you agree, darling?" 🌿

The ancient valley oak, Quercus lobata, *fronting the home of Francis and Eleanor, has a longer history even than the Niebaum estate. Broad verandahs are the scene of many summer gatherings.*

OPPOSITE: *The Coppolas' garden is filled with floral delights through-out the year, including this peony.*

PERHAPS IT'S THE RETREATS THAT ELEANOR COPPOLA HOSTS IN THIS GARDEN THAT engender such a sense of tranquillity and peace here. Although this is a rather complex garden, the overriding feeling is one of serenity. I find myself wanting to sit quietly on the large extended porch and read, or wander through the paths, marveling at the gigantic hundred-foot-tall oaks and feeling a part of another era—a grander, gentler era—the era of Gustave Niebaum, who originally put in the extensive gardens.

There are many wonderful stories about the fastidious Captain Niebaum, who was known for his surprise white glove inspections in the winery. Lore tells us he insisted his long driveway be swept daily, from the main highway to his house (almost a quarter of a mile). The same attention to detail can still be seen in the grand Victorian house designed in 1888 by Albert Shroepper. Special woods and craftsmen were brought from Europe to complete the project.

But Niebaum's love of perfection was not limited to winemaking, buildings, or managing. He loved nature, and he so respected the old trees on his property that he would not allow any to be removed, even for his vineyard.

So, quite naturally, he planned the house and the garden around the four-hundred-year-old oaks. The design of the garden is a typical Victorian layout, a curved driveway circling an expansive, stone-edged lawn. The tall, ancient oaks provide not only shade, but also create a sense of liveliness, with ever-changing patterns of light on the smooth green grass below. Informal gravel footpaths lead around planted areas to the greenhouse, vegetable garden, pond, and rose cottage. In Niebaum's time, the garden required thirteen gardeners to maintain it, and included a state-of-the-art stable, horses, chickens, pigs, and cows, often producing enough extra to sell.

Luckily, all of the subsequent owners appreciated and cherished both the home and garden and left them much the way Niebaum had designed them, simply paring down to fit into today's style of living. Two subsequent owners

PREVIOUS PAGES: *Mirroring*

the idyllic and tranquil beauty of

the Coppola estate, a swan glides

across the guest house pond from

one Japanese maple to the other.

ABOVE: *The glasshouse provides*

shelter for house plants and emerg-

ing seedlings. RIGHT: *Dogwood*

flanks the stone stairway, which

originally led to the carriage house.

RIGHT: *Looking at these splendid old gardens with their old-fashioned bulbs and enormous ancient trees makes us realize that in our lifetime we could not create such a place.*

BELOW: *Bell-like blossoms of scilla.*

were particularly good custodians: Elizabeth Daniels and her husband, John Daniels, Niebaum's grand nephew, who lived on the estate from 1936 to 1971, and Jean Van Lobensels, who made her home there from 1971 to 1975. As Elizabeth's daughter, Robin Lail, tells it, her mother put her heart into the four-acre grounds, maintaining them with a considerably smaller staff than Niebaum. She continued a slightly smaller vegetable garden, and added fruit trees, copper beeches, and Japanese maples, now all exquisite specimens. Jean Van Lobensels was also a great gardener, adding lots of annuals, a few perennials, and reducing the cultivated areas a bit.

Eleanor Coppola has a different relationship to the gardens. Though she does not garden herself, she considers the garden her soul. "It constantly sustains and inspires me," Eleanor says. "I need to be in the garden every day. It grounds me, adding that inner harmony." And that's what this garden expresses—strength, grace, and harmony.

The Coppolas have updated the garden with an automatic sprinkler system that improves water efficiency. Bay Area landscape designer Sarah Hammond is now consulting Eleanor on new planting areas.

Springtime is breathtaking here when the blue scilla appears in many of the hedged beds and other bulbs erupt in glory, while cherry blossoms fill the horizon. Then just as these spring phenomena end, large dogwoods direct your attention to the other side of the garden and to an all-but-forgotten stone slab stairway leading down to the lower level and the old carriage house. These dramatic, broad stairs provided the main entrance for guests in Niebaum's time.

Today, besides the meditative qualities of the garden, there's a wonderful sense of life. Francis's love of theater, food, and cooking can be clearly seen in the restaurant-sized pizza oven behind the house, near the kitchen where he loves to cook and entertain. So this estate has become a retreat, haven, workplace, and play place for Francis and Eleanor Coppola, their children, and their friends. ☙

OLD WORLD, NEW WORLD

HOW TO LINK THE OLD WITH THE NEW? GARDENS IN THIS SECTION

HAVE SUCCESSFULLY DONE SO, STARTING WITH BUILDINGS THAT

DATE FROM THE LATE 1800S TO THE 1930S. WHILE TREES AND SHRUBS

ARE OFTEN WELL OVER A HUNDRED YEARS OLD, THE PRESENT OWN-

ERS HAVE ADDED COMPLEMENTARY NEW GARDENS.

PREVIOUS PAGES: *Late afternoon*

sunlight filters through Chotsie

Blank's rose garden. OPPOSITE:

Chotsie's inspired arrangement of

heurchera, sweet peas, delphinium,

and roses from her garden. THIS

PAGE: *An aerial view of "Villa*

Insteada" shows its relation to sur-

rounding vineyards, and helps us

appreciate the selection of trees

made years ago by Thomas Church.

A honeysuckle vine envelopes the

tool house, while Allan's bamboo

sculpture lends interest to the rose

garden entrance.

NO MATTER WHAT TIME OF YEAR OR DAY ONE VISITS Chotsie Blank's garden, it is superb. For a gardener to create a place that looks wonderful at all times is a miracle, and only someone who knows how to delegate and still be involved could accomplish it at all. Perhaps it's those qualities that have made Chotsie so valuable to the San Francisco Museum of Modern Art, where she currently serves as chair of the Architecture and Design Forum.

Allan and Chotsie Blank moved here from Chicago nineteen years ago, with hopes of making wine. But land prices had risen so rapidly that the dream became unfeasible. They fell in love with the Valley anyway, and found this property. Thus they lovingly dubbed their new home Villa Insteada, "insteada" a winery.

When they took possession of the property, Chotsie decided the area that had been used as a pumpkin patch would be an ideal location for a formal rose garden. And, sure enough, roses now bloom there in abundance. The rose garden is not just a collection of plants; it is a knowledgeable *selection* of some of the most beautiful and fragrant roses to be found: climbers, ramblers, hybrid teas, damasks, old-fashioneds, and miniatures, all in harmonizing colors. Woven into this magnificent tapestry of color and fragrance are ground covers in exquisite combinations, along with pleasing color waves of penstemon, foxglove, and salvia.

This is a fairy tale rose garden—lush plots encircling an ancient-looking, deep fountain, all enclosed in white lattice with a welcoming arch and a low gate that allows you to peek in before entering. As you do enter, you see, you smell, you *feel* roses. Their fragrances are as distinctive as their colors— colors of white, cream, peach, apricot, pink, a deeper pink, and pale gold.

Originally, Chotsie consulted with landscaper, Sarah Hammond, to help design the rose garden. It turned out splendidly, but then disaster struck: "Just when the roses got established," Chotsie says, drawing a deep breath, "we had a terrible attack of oak root fungus. All the roses were dying." That meant fumigating the soil, taking up the brick paths, and starting all over.

The Blanks asked Napa Valley horticulturist and designer Roger Warner for his advice on the makeover. Roger concurred with Chotsie's desire for a slightly stronger palette. He gave more color *and* a bit more structure to the new garden, adding

four pillars in the middle of each plot and covering them with 'Fantin-Latour' roses. "I thought he was crazy at first," Chotsie says, "because they were just big wooden posts. But in springtime, they're really a sight, covered with big, deep pink blossoms." And while there are more extensive plantings of roses in the Napa Valley, none surpass the effect that has been created here.

Another part of the property, equally attractive from a serious cook's standpoint, is what Chotsie calls her "insurance garden"—herbs for the kitchen and cut flowers for luxuriant indoor bouquets. Eight rectangular, raised beds, varying in height and size, are contained within a larger square, producing a rhythmic sense of order. "Some people see the herb garden and say, 'Oh, this is even better than the roses!'" Chotsie says with a smile. "It's more natural and takes its own shape and form." In one bed is a terra-cotta urn with the face of a lion peering regally from beneath overflowing herbs. Once the top of the fountain in the rose garden, the urn interrupted the view from the entrance, so it found a new life among the herbs. And here too, roses have crept in—cabbage-sized tea roses in strong shades of apricot line the perimeter.

Chotsie has incorporated every aspect of the property into the garden scheme: she enveloped the lath pump house with a climbing 'Iceberg' rose and another lath tool house with honeysuckle. Rows of pale apricot daylilies connect the driveway to the rose garden. Areas which were neutral have become important connective links through the introduction of a continuous low-growing boxwood hedge; the entire decomposed granite driveway is now integrated into the landscape.

"I try to keep the transition areas in the same palette as the main garden around the house," Chotsie says, "so even though there are many sections to this garden, it flows."

"Gardening is learning," she explains. "When we started gardening here, I was told that peonies wouldn't grow in this climate, but they're doing beautifully. Or just when you think you've got everything down pat, along comes a gopher or something and it forces you to start all over. But no matter what, the garden gives me special pleasure. I love having a ready supply of floral materials to decorate our home. Branches, roses, whatever—there's never a need to buy anything. And I have plenty to share with friends." ❦

PREVIOUS PAGES: Arched gates and broad paths invite us into this charming rose garden, a showcase for Old World varieties. The predominantly pink palette is greatly enhanced by punctuations of strong purples—Campanula persicifolia, Baptisia australis 'Purple', the low-growing Teucrium, and Nepeta—around the fountain. ABOVE: As storm clouds approach, subtle shifts in light play upon the vineyard, Matilija poppies, and the David Austin rose 'Othello' near the herb garden. OPPOSITE: An herb garden montage includes golden sage, several thymes, lavenders, flowering chives, alliums, artichokes, campanula, 'Sour Grape' penstemon, and roses and tulips at the exit gate. Brimming over the edge of some of the raised beds is one of my favorite plants, the dwarf oregano.

THE IDEAL WAY TO VISIT A NAPA VALLEY ESTATE GARDEN IS BY HORSE AND CARRIAGE. When Ron and Joanne Birtcher enlisted the help of Napa landscape architect Steve Arns for the renovation at Meadowbrook Farm, they had that concept clearly in mind. Arns retained the original nineteenth-century carriage trails that were on the property and extended them in several directions, adding a cottage garden close to the house, two large ponds connected by a stream, recreational areas, and more informal plantings over four acres.

In hackney pony and quarter horse circles, the Birtchers are widely known for their expertise, so from the start Arns's concept was to provide plenty of space for that recreation, as well as to express the Birtchers' love of flowers. This is a path and trail garden, with lots of different areas to discover and explore—on foot or, better yet, in a horse-drawn antique carriage. Shady trails lead past classic statuary the Birtchers have collected from all over the world. Arns has masterfully introduced woodland plants such as azaleas, camellias, astilbes, and hostas into the natural, predominantly oak forest, providing subtle seasonal color along quiet, creekside carriageways and walkways. The trails continue to wind all the way around the property and among the farm's outbuildings, one of which has been converted into a combination stable and private museum for the family's unique carriage collection.

The Birtchers, their children, and grandchildren all love the farm and feel a part of the history of the Napa Valley when the horse is hitched up to the shining black carriage that carries them through the shady creek-bed trail. ❦

OPPOSITE: *The one-hundred-year-old carriage trails have been reinstated with selective woodland planting, creating a completely natural appearance.* ABOVE: *Several wings of the rambling country house open onto outdoor living areas. The western terrace, center, is near the stream bed and the carriage trail. Chartreuse moss–covered bricks provide a handsome entrance beneath the double barn doors of the carriage house.*

OPPOSITE: *Bill Jaeger brilliantly*

used metal hoops from wooden

tanks to form the graceful rose-

covered arch leading from the gar-

den through the vineyard to the

pond. THIS PAGE: Clematis

lawsoniana *'Henryi', with its*

huge white flowers, and the fra-

grant Clematis montana

'Rubens' mingle as they reach for

the top of the locust tree. Lila

descends the steps of the verandah

to follow the path toward the arbor

of 'Blaze' roses and grapevines.

NO MATTER HOW HARD WE TRY TO KEEP A GARDEN IN A permanent state of beauty, Mother Nature is always in a state of transition, engaging in constant relandscaping whether we like it or not.

At Inglewood, the Napa Valley home of Bill and Lila Jaeger, this fact of life became heartrendingly clear in March 1996. The Jaegers were out of town and received a telephone call from their son in the Valley: "I have very sad news for you," he said. "You've lost two of your dearest friends. Both over one hundred years old."

"I couldn't imagine whom he meant," Lila recalls as her eyes wander to a distant part of the garden. "Then he said, 'The ponderosas.'"

The towering ponderosa pines, a focal point between the Jaegers' yellow Victorian and their picturesque guest house, were toppled by sixty-mile-per-hour winds. Cabled together, they crashed through roses, a beautiful *Magnolia stellata*, garden furniture, a fountain, and numerous shrubs. They uprooted a nearby locust and landed with such force that one branch was driven twelve feet into the lawn. "I cried all the way home from Chicago," Lila recalls.

Six weeks later, a visitor would have had little idea of the devastation caused by the storm. Where the trees once stood is a flower bed that looks as if it were planned from the start, and the main house and guest house now appear to be closer together than before.

After "weekending" in the Valley for five years, the permanent move for the Jaegers came about in 1970, when Bill was offered a partnership in Freemark Abbey Winery. At the time, the landscaping on the twelve-acre parcel (eight in vineyard) was minimal, but the property was blessed with beautiful old oaks, maples, and ponderosa pines and had excellent drainage for future expansion. The most important assets, however, were the Jaegers themselves, two avid gardeners who hired San Francisco landscape architect Ernest Wertheim to develop a long-range plan.

"He was wonderful," Lila says. "He interviewed every member of the family, asking each of us what we wanted the garden to be." As a result, the newly landscaped area became delightfully serviceable for them all—from accommodating Lila's needs for a flower garden, to providing plenty of recreational areas for their teenagers.

Like two cooks in the same kitchen, Bill and Lila occasionally found they had different visions about the development of the garden. "Sometimes," Lila

PREVIOUS PAGES: *Dark green native digger pines provide a rich backdrop for the light yellow poplar trees edging the pond.* ABOVE: *A tennis court serves a dual function when the fence becomes a trellis for roses.* LEFT: *Reflections are half the enjoyment of a water garden. At one end of the pond, Bill chose the strong architectural repeat of poplar trees; at the other are colorful composites and pink 'Meidiland' roses.*

laughs, "Bill would tell the gardener what to do, then I'd tell him something different . . . and the poor man was getting confused." So Bill concentrated his talents on the areas around the tennis court and the rose arbor, and he took on the sizable task of landscaping around the small lake that they had created in a joint venture with next-door neighbors. The result is amazing. A row of poplars breaks up the skyline, and their reflections, along with those of the roses at the opposite end of the pond, create a magical place at dawn and sunset. No one would suspect an amateur had designed this enchanting pond.

Around the house, Lila first determined to plant strictly perennials, except for the handsome hanging baskets combining variegated ivy and coral impatiens. "But in a garden this big I really needed a splash of color," she says. "I had to have petunias and pansies. They give that needed *oomph* at a time when the perennials are quiet."

One of the nicest features of old California Victorian homes such as the Jaegers' is the large verandah. These porches, usually set about four feet above ground level, offer a good view of the surroundings. In the Jaegers' case, the view originally was of cars and pickups. Wertheim rerouted the driveway, established a lawn and flower beds where the old one had been, and camouflaged the new parking area with trees and shrubs.

As the garden evolved, other landscape designers were consulted. Catherine Matthewson added Italian cypress, which gave the garden greater depth. Sarah Hammond, the creator of the nursery at Smith and Hawken, contributed a lovely softening effect around the pool with plantings of *Euphorbia* x *martinii*, *Campanula persicifolia*, *Teucrium*, low-growing rosemary, erigeron, lavender, and lots of cranesbill geraniums. Plants like these have contributed a more contemporary feeling than the strictly old-fashioned Victorian gardens have.

Looking out from the solarium, her favorite room after the kitchen, Lila says she enjoys the view of the garden without suffering guilt about jobs that ought to be done. "I'm not a perfectionist gardener. No way. I garden for enjoyment!" ❦

RIGHT: *Red-tipped stamens give a dark accent to the large white petals of the* Clematis lawsoniana *'Henryi'.* LEFT: *Landscape consultant Sarah Hammond selected the plants for these graceful borders. Standard 'Graham Thomas' roses rise out of clipped mounds of* Santolina virens, *with 'Iceberg' roses in the distance. Front edging is* Erigeron karvinskianus *and the back is* Nepeta mussinii.

RIGHT: *Loving the filtered light of the tall oaks,* Campanula persicifolia *'Telham Beauty' blooms profusely along with the* Geranium cantabrigiense *'Biokovo' and* Lavandula angustifolia.

ABOVE: *The beautifully restored Far Niente Winery.* ABOVE RIGHT: *Patterned bark of River Birch* (Betula nigra 'Heritage'). BELOW: *A*

simple planting of olives adds to the quiet mood of winter. OPPOSITE: *A majestic moss-covered oak is enhanced by an elaborate underplanting*

of Loropetalum chinense, *white* Phlox subulata, *'Pink Ruffle' azaleas, and the fragrant* Rhododendron maddenii.

ANYONE VISITING THE FAR NIENTE WINERY, WITH ITS THIRTEEN ACRES OF FORMAL gardens, might be led to believe that the historic stone winery has always been as beautiful as it is now. But when Oklahoma nurseryman Gil Nickel bought the property in 1979, its major attraction was an abandoned stone building whose only use in recent years had been as a party site for local teenagers.

Now listed on the National Register of Historic Places, the old winery building has been turned into a lavish, tastefully furnished winery with slate floors on two levels and hand-rubbed oak planks in Nickel's third-floor offices. The caves that Nickel had dug beneath the building provide twenty-seven thousand square feet of space for the careful maturation of Cabernet, Chardonnay, and Far Niente's premium dessert wine, Dolce, reminding us of that wonderful Italian phrase *dolce far niente*—"how sweet to do nothing."

As owner of America's third largest wholesale nursery (Greenleaf, with growing grounds in North Carolina, Texas, and Oklahoma), Nickel made it a priority to landscape the winery, as well as the adjacent redwood barn that houses his collection of classic automobiles and boats, with a great deal of care. In 1988 Nickel shared his dream of establishing a world-class garden with landscape architect Jonathan Plant, who cheerfully accepted the challenge.

Plant earned a degree in horticulture from the Royal Botanic Gardens in Kew, England, before returning to manage the native plant collections at U.C. Berkeley's botanical garden. He says he was further inspired by working with a client who had the horticultural knowledge and wherewithal to make his dreams happen. Instead of plants being purchased by the flat, they arrived by the truckload from Oklahoma and Texas.

The entry drive leads past a part of the garden known as the Great Savannah—seven acres of heritage oaks, native bunchgrasses, daffodils, and wildflowers that serve to heighten expectations of what will be seen beyond the winery's entrance. Just inside the black wrought iron gates is a four-acre woodland garden where more than seven thousand azaleas (perhaps the largest single planting in California) blend with native oaks on the quick-draining hillside. Like many legendary English gardens, this one appears magically to have just "happened," but it is actually the result of meticulous planning and planting.

In addition to valley oaks, blue oaks, live oaks, white oaks, cork oaks, and the redwoods and olive trees, the garden showcases significant specimen trees such as Japanese maple (*Acer palmatum*), Japanese snowbell (*Styrax japonicus*), and saucer magnolia (*Magnolia* x *soulangeana*).

As Plant points out, Nickel has constantly urged moderation in the landscape. "It's not all razzle-dazzle, but like grounds designed in the European tradition, where restraint is used in massive plantings. It's an estate garden, meant to accentuate an appreciation for wine in a beautiful setting." 🌿

LEFT: *Sunlit moss emphasizes the sculptural branches of the magnificent centuries-old oak. The dappled light below is exactly what the azaleas and rhododendrons need. Consistent pruning, done religiously twice a year, is required of the trees above as well as the azaleas below. New growth is tipped to expose more flowers. After flowering, bushes are sheared to keep plants compact.*

RIGHT: *Napa Valley fog adds much-needed moisture to grapes and azaleas alike. Young 'Autumn Gold'* Ginkgo biloba *strive to take their place with the native walnut along the quiet entrance drive. Dripping Spanish moss forms a graceful canopy over mounds and mounds of pastel azaleas as far as the eye can see. A hydro-seeded bank of flax, poppies,* Brodiaea, *and baby blue eyes produces this dazzling effect.*

OPPOSITE: *Katie Trefethen's gardener, David Alosi, tends to seasonal chores in the perennial border.* ABOVE: *A bird's eye view of Katie's garden, which used to serve as an outdoor classroom for her garden classes. In recent years her interest has turned to bonsai.*

ABOVE RIGHT: *Foo dogs guard the quiet front entrance where most of the color appears in spring with blooming bulbs, irises, dogwood, peonies, and hellebores.*

KATIE TREFETHEN'S PLANT COLLECTION IS A REGIONAL resource for any serious wine country gardener. Every available inch of ground is home to some unusual plant or other. And when Katie opens her garden to the public, docents are on hand to pass out lists of some of the twelve hundred extraordinary plants to be found in various areas of the landscape.

The Trefethen garden has its roots in the last century. The winery, established in 1886, is one of the oldest in the Valley. It's not, however, the vintage design or even the plant selections that make this garden memorable; it is Katie Trefethen's personality that comes through—her enthusiasm, her curiosity, her generosity. These are qualities difficult to capture in photographs, but unmistakable when you are in her garden.

A sense of adventure is found everywhere. Katie's tastes are broad and eclectic. It takes courage, artistry, and great self-confidence to paint the winery and huge barns orange and then to trim the main house in the same color, outlined with the kind of purple you see in spring delphinium.

And as for Katie's humor, well, all you need is a stroll through her statuary and her collection of chickens. Her affection encompasses everything in the garden—plants, butterflies, birds, all living things both wild in her pond and domestic in her cages—and everything man-made. Whimsy is found in every path with the sudden encounter of a strange dog statue or a two-foot ceramic goose. It's those kinds of surprises, along with her dynamic horticultural assemblage, that make Katie's garden such a delightful place.

She has a very simple explanation for the wealth and diversity of plant material that surrounds her home: "I'm just a passionate gardener. Every peony, every hellebore, dogwood, clematis, hydrangea, and salvia means something to me."

When the Trefethens purchased this home in Napa in 1968, Katie was overjoyed at the prospect of having her "very own country garden." Renovation on the two-story structure and construction of a swimming pool began right away, but it wasn't until several years later that they called in Piedmont, California, landscape architect Floyd Mick to help lay out the garden.

Palm trees that had surrounded the house were removed because Katie thought tropical trees were out of place in Northern California. But seeing how well some old orange trees were doing, they decided to line a new, rerouted driveway with rows of citrus. (Originally, the main entrance came directly off the highway.) They also planted Italian cypress, which supplied badly needed verticals that helped interrupt the flatness of the land, and coastal redwoods, which provided protection from daily afternoon winds.

Katie's Garden

PREVIOUS PAGES: *Perhaps Katie's favorite view of her garden is this one from the back terrace, where the importance of the vertical cypresses is revealed as they throw slender diagonal shadows across the lawn.* LEFT: *The rose arbor with 'Climbing America' mirrors Mrs. Trefethen's artistic sensibilities.* BELOW: *A ceramic rooster frozen in mid-crow adds a sense of whimsy.* OPPOSITE: *The photo montage shows the eclectic diversity of a garden that includes rhododendrons, clematis, yellow Fremontia, peonies, daylilies, wisteria, valerian, quince, and statuary.*

The garden has evolved since Mick's original plan. Indeed, part of the nature of Katie's garden is change. Advice from landscape architect Mai Arbegast of Berkeley has had a good deal of influence in both design and plant selection. "I'm able to give Katie some input along the way," Mai demurs, "but it's very much her garden."

A design element that attracts considerable attention from students of garden design is the row of five seven-foot-tall pillars at the front edge of the perennial English border, stationed like sentries and bedecked with roses. "Penelope Hobhouse was visiting from England one day," Katie recalls, "and this was her idea as a solution for what to do with this area."

For someone who loves plants and gardening and is so knowledgeable about them, it is surprising to learn that Katie has no formal education in botany. Instead, she attributes her ability to design a garden to her background in art. "Color combinations are second nature to me," she says. "Shapes and patterns are what I've studied all my life."

And Katie has passed along that knowledge, as well as a good bit of straightforward horticultural advice, to those who have taken part in her informal gardening classes. "It was easy to teach in the beginning," she laughs, "because nobody knew anything about gardening in those days. Anything I said, they'd write down. But it's not so easy today."

Although never one to worry about having dirt under her fingernails, Katie acknowledges that her advancing years have had an impact on what she wants to do, and what she is able to do. "The thing is, I'm too old to get down on the ground anymore," she says with a look of mock dismay, "so I have David Alosi maintain the garden, and I have my bonsai trees in containers and get my hands dirty that way."

Besides the tell-tale sign of hands that actually touch earth, Katie has one other measure of sensibility: "I've always been impatient with gardeners who insist that the garden be in bloom before they let you look around. I love my garden even when *nothing's* blooming. What's wrong with green?" ❦

63

ABOVE: *Even the interior of the garden shed is alive, thanks to a Virginia creeper vine.* RIGHT: *A bonsai wisteria "allows me to keep dirt under my fingernails," Katie says. This male peacock is among the many birds that call her garden home.*

One structure in the garden that always draws comments is the two-story metal gazebo. A spiral staircase leads visitors to the "bird cage" observation platform—a fine place for an overview of the house, garden, surrounding vineyards, and these delightful fruit trees. Bronze magnolia leaves give contrast to Blue Star Creeper (Isotoma/ Laurentia fluviatilis) ground cover.

THE LINK FROM CLASSICAL TO CONTEMPORARY: THOMAS CHURCH GARDENS

LANDSCAPE ARCHITECT THOMAS D. CHURCH (1902-1978) IS WIDELY

HAILED AS THE ORIGINATOR OF THE MODERN CALIFORNIA GAR-

DEN. HIS LANDMARK BOOK *GARDENS ARE FOR PEOPLE* ADVOCATED

CAREFUL SITING AND ORIENTATION OF HOUSE AND GARDEN WITH

EXISTING TREES AND TOPOGRAPHY. ❋ AT FIRST GLANCE, HIS GAR-

DENS MAY NOT SEEM PEOPLE-ORIENTED OR PARTICULARLY

FRIENDLY, BECAUSE OF THEIR FORMALITY. BUT CHURCH WAS A

MASTER AT INCORPORATING FAMILY REQUIREMENTS INTO THE

OVERALL GARDEN PLAN. ENTRANCE DRIVES, PARKING, GARAGE,

STORAGE, AND ENTERTAINING AREAS HAVE ALL BEEN HAND-

SOMELY ADDRESSED. ❋ THE THREE NAPA VALLEY GARDENS HERE,

INSTALLED FROM 1938 TO 1972, SERVE AS BENCHMARKS IN THOMAS

CHURCH'S ILLUSTRIOUS CAREER.

PREVIOUS PAGE: *Meticulously clipped hedges in the Phillipses' garden*

illustrate one of Church's devices for defining space and creating order. THIS

PAGE: *A strong underlying structure is also apparent in this early Church*

garden. Here the hedges enclose and repeat the rectangular shape of the pool.

A cement walkway creates an axis from the terrace to the rest of the garden,

traversing the pool.

THE FIRST OF THE GARDENS, COMPLETED IN 1938, NESTLES behind the handsome and comfortable home where Dick and I visited nonagenarian Alice Gonser, who has lived there with her family for forty-one years. The garden is such a part of the property it looks as if it were installed when the formidable stone building was erected in 1876 to serve as a winery.

Instead of the clipped boxwood hedges and gravel pathways which became a Thomas Church trademark later in his career, Mrs. Gonser's garden is simplicity itself, with junipers crowning the stone walls that edge the drive and lawn. A stone stairway in the middle of the wall invites you to a small, secluded area perfect for meditation or viewing the activities below. Large, old olive trees flank the stone entrance to the pool and lawn area. Plantings of an olive orchard above the stone wall, a vineyard, a stately laurel hedge, and a towering Irish yew add structural landmarks. ❦

I never know whether it's the sweet

perfume, the bending form, or

the light beaming through the white

blossoms that is most appealing

about the wisteria tree that draws

us into Bob and Alex's garden.

THE "MYSTERY GARDEN," INSTALLED AT VINEHILL RANCH IN 1959 AT THE HEIGHT OF Church's career, is now owned by Bob and Alex Phillips. As Alex explains, Church had already created two gardens for her parents in San Francisco, but for some reason there was a falling out between landscaper and owner when the upper level of the garden was being developed. For a long time a stone stairway, reminiscent of the one at Mrs. Gonser's, led from the gravel parking area only to a thicket of trees and underbrush. It fell to the Phillipses to continue landscaping without intruding upon Church's creation, and it's quite likely he would have applauded their efforts as a celebration of outdoor living.

Over a seasonal stream in a wooded area, Alex's father had created a Japanese spirit bridge (juxtaposed planks arranged so a person being followed by a bothersome spirit can jump to one side while the spirit—who can travel only in a straight line—tumbles off the edge). The bridge encouraged traveling uphill, but dead-ended in a tangle of scrub oaks.

Then one day Bob explored the trees and said, "Maybe there's a pond in here." And that set wheels in motion. Landscape Architect Jack Chandler was hired to "discover" the pond, which suddenly gave Church's stairway a destination. From there, work on the hillside continued, with the result that the wild garden and formal garden blend seamlessly.

Still, there's no doubt that the rest of the landscape simply serves as an entree to Church's handiwork. At the Phillipses', as in many of his creations, the swimming pool is a focal point in a symmetrical garden. Church's pools are always beautifully proportioned, have some architectural detail, and often are a major feature in the landscape.

A master at directing the eye, Church has placed the pool on an axis with the house to draw your vision straight out beyond the garden to views of the distant vineyards and hills. His restraint and superb proportions produce a landscape that is elegant and serene.

As Alex puts it, "We really didn't know anything about gardening, but this is so easy to maintain because it's laid out simply. Except for shaping the hedges, Bob and I do all the gardening ourselves. In the summer, having just the color green is cool and lovely. I suppose if one wanted, they could take out the hedges and put in roses, but that's not what we want."

And in respect for the landscape, Alex has become a true gardener: "You become entranced by gardening and have to try different things. I'm always spotting something in a nursery and bringing it home. It's irresistible. I spend as much time moving things around as I do enjoying the looks of them. In fall or winter you have time to think, 'Maybe this would be better over there,' and it usually is."

Alex credits much of her love for gardening with being a charter member of Katie Trefethen's class: "I remember when she called and invited me to join. She said it was not going to be a garden club, because that's too democratic. Katie said, 'It will be a class and I'm going to teach it!' I was only too happy to join," Alex recalls, "since I knew nothing about gardening at the time. So it's been a great learning experience and I've really been in the grip of a garden passion ever since." ❦

Strongly Italianate in appearance,

the pool, on axis with the house,

carries the eye out across the garden

to the vineyards beyond. Floating

garlands in a geometric pattern

for a wedding ceremony repeat the

rectangular theme of the garden

hedges in the pool and recapitulate

the classical beauty. Years of

skillful pruning have resulted in

this arresting fig tree sculpture.

LEFT: *The disjointed planks of this beguiling Japanese "spirit bridge" lead toward the pond, which the Phillipses added to the landscape. A sunburst locust glorifies this peaceful setting in spring.* BELOW: *Bob's magnificent undulating vineyard stretching up to meet the heavily wooded foothills creates the perfect "borrowed landscape."* RIGHT: *The entrance drive reminds us of the stone wall with clipped junipers at Mrs. Gonser's.*

THE THIRD GARDEN WAS BUILT IN 1972 ON A VINEYARD PROMONTORY, AGAINST CHURCH'S advice. He had wanted the site moved to a more protected location, but the owners, Virginia and Jerry Draper, were enthralled with the commanding views in all directions, and vetoed the landscaper's suggestion. Thus, the home and garden were built on one level.

After his parents' deaths, son Jerry and his wife Norma Draper, always appreciative of the family home, became the residents and guardians of this lovely property.

The garden's shape is primarily determined by that of the French country house and is divided into two rooms, defined by trees arranged at the edges. "The axis runs through both house and garden," explains Susan Britton, a landscape architect who, as a graduate student at the University of California at Davis, wrote a paper that featured the Draper property. "Literally, you open the front door of the courtyard and there in front of you is the garden and reflecting pool with a view of the vineyards beyond."

Though formal, the garden's dominant theme is one of simplicity. One side of the pool is flanked by rows of trees outlined by very low concrete walls. Clipped star jasmine (*Trachelospermum jasminoides*) grows inside the masonry. On the other side of the pool, towards the valley view, is a rounded green lawn with a large chestnut tree. Farther around, outside the French doors of the dining room, is a handsome, round, sunken garden lined with Italian alders. "I'm not sure what the original purpose was," said Norma, "but we use it as our outdoor dining room. It's great for that!" Once again the axis is carried from the house, this time from the dining room through the sunken gravel circle to a break in the long, low retaining wall, allowing a view of the tops of grapes and distant hills.

The contrast between this garden and the 1938 Gonser garden shows the development of the Thomas Church style: a style that was always graceful, but that became very pure, more refined, almost minimalist—and even more graceful. 🌿

Church's masterful use of proportion gives lasting harmony to transient gardens. OPPOSITE: *Formal yet welcoming, Church's graceful curving walkways invite us to explore further.* ABOVE: *Large double doors open from the courtyard. The vista of the symmetrical Italian Cypresses around the pool reflects Church's classical training. Imitating the manicured hedges are curving stone walls.* LEFT: *A sunken recreation area is outlined by Italian alders.*

WE BEGIN OUR DATING OF NEW GARDENS AROUND 1960. IT'S CURIOUS THAT JUST ABOUT A HUNDRED YEARS AFTER THE FIRST FAMILIES SETTLED HERE, NEWCOMERS BEGAN APPEARING ONCE AGAIN TO TRY THEIR SKILL AT WINEMAKING. IN THE NAPA VALLEY, WINEMAKING IS NOT AN ISOLATED ART FORM, BUT IS PART OF THE FABRIC OF GRACIOUS LIVING WHICH INCLUDES THE ARTS OF COOKING, HOMEMAKING, AND GARDENING, ALONG WITH APPRECIATION OF MUSIC, LITERATURE, AND THE VISUAL ARTS. ❄ VINTNERS ARE BASICALLY FARMERS, AND IT IS NATURAL THAT THEIR FARM-ING WOULD EXTEND TO GARDENING—FOR BEAUTY AS WELL AS SUSTENANCE. THESE RECENT GARDENS REFLECT OWNERS WHO ARE OPEN TO THE TRADITIONS OF THE PAST, AND YET ARE WILLING TO TRY NEW IDEAS, CREATING NEW FRONTIERS.

NEW
GARDENS

EUROPEAN INFLUENCES IN NEW GARDENS

JUST AS IN THE EARLY GARDENS OF THE NAPA VALLEY, TODAY'S

GARDENS OFTEN SHOW STRONG EUROPEAN INFLUENCES. BOTH

THE CUNNINGHAMS' AND THE HUDSONS' FAVORITE GARDENS

WERE IN ITALY. THE WILSEYS WERE IMPRESSED BY THE TULIP

DISPLAYS IN AMSTERDAM. THE FISHERS WERE DRAWN TO THE

HOMES AND GARDENS OF NORMANDY.

PREVIOUS PAGES: *Grasses and Russian sage at the Araujos'; Annie Fisher's Normandy chateau.*

OPPOSITE: *Stone pillars twined in grapevines with ivy accents at the base lend an air of classical formality to the Cunningham villa, where K.C. expands horizons, above.*

WHEN K.C. CUNNINGHAM HEARS HERSELF DESCRIBED AS A born-again gardener, she laughs and nods her head in agreement. "I am. This has been my passion for three years, and my husband says I spend more time in the garden than with him."

The seven-year-old home was a modern version of Southwest architecture when Jerry and K.C. purchased the property, and the garden, which had been designed by Jack Chandler, was going into decline.

"The Napa Valley doesn't seem like the Southwest to me," K.C. explains. "It seems more like Italy."

Massive redecoration took place indoors to create the ambience of a Tuscan villa, with the walls and beamed ceiling of the living room painted with floral motifs by reknowned artist Carlo Marchiori. Windows were enlarged and new views of the garden were added, erasing the dividing line between house and garden.

Enlisting the talents of plantsman Jay Hoover, the Cunninghams began the makeover of the garden. "We tore out everything except the hedges and started over," K.C. explains. With a clear idea in mind, they have created a garden with purpose and beauty which, although young at this point, portends greatness.

Formality and order, trademarks of the garden, are apparent the moment you enter the driveway. A stone balustrade and tall cypresses give us an Italian greeting.

One of the most striking areas of the garden is the parterre. The geometric pattern of clipped box hedge squares surrounds plantings of the low-growing, profusely blooming white 'Meidiland' roses, accented by oversized pots of citrus that emphasize the Italian flavor. Looking out from the parterre and from the verandah above, we see an enormous flat, green lawn that invites a stroll to the other side, where mounds of perennials act as a gentle buffer before the grand view of adjacent vineyards.

Each area of the garden presented special problems, because of heavy clay soil. "We took out truckloads of it when we redid the lawn," K.C. sighs. "We've also improved the soil with compost that recycles all of the grass clippings from the lawn, which covers about an acre."

But even now the property, situated near the Napa River, is subject to some flooding. The house is spared because it is built on an eight-foot-high berm. "We'd be severely flooded if it weren't for Jack Chandler's brilliance," K.C. acknowledges, "and when it does flood, the water enters one corner of the property, goes through that swale, and out the other side. It just deposits some silt and really doesn't harm the lawn."

"I'm planning to go on gardening for a long time," K.C. remarks, "so we've put in waist-high raised vegetable beds. We call it our 'senior bed'—none of us has to bend over for harvest!"

OPPOSITE: *The geometry of the parterre is nicely emphasized by the elongated rectangular pool and Jacuzzi. Tightly trimmed boxwood encloses lavenders and white 'Meidiland' roses with enormous terra-cotta pots of citrus trees and white lantana.* RIGHT: *Simplicity distinguishes this quiet courtyard at the entrance to the parterre. The rounded boxwood, 'Winter Gem',* at the base of the Chinese hackberry trees (Celtis sinensis) *is softened by* Erigeron karvinskianus *and pelargoniums.* BELOW: *A stepped lawn area defined by a singular stone edging adds a subtle sense of unity, order, and beauty to this young garden.*

The colors and plants of the South-

west enliven the home and gardens

of Lee and Becky Hudson. The

Hudsons' garden is both formal

and casual, with a very effective

use of texture. The spined leaves of

Agave americana, *above,*

become an architectural element,

as does flowering Yucca fila-

mentosa, *opposite.*

ON TOP OF A HILL OVERLOOKING SAN FRANCISCO BAY IS A GARDEN THAT SHOUTS WITH vitality, variety, and originality. It fulfills all the qualities that Hugh Johnson, in his book *The Principles of Gardening,* says should be apparent in a good garden: ". . . a plan, with variety but consistency, with a firm sense of purpose so that you know where to look, and what you are supposed to enjoy."

With backgrounds in horticulture, viticulture, and art, Lee and Becky Hudson were well prepared to create a magnificent garden. Becky, vivacious and self-effacing, notes that many people were involved in its creation: Sonoma architect Ned Forrest, New York interior designer Mark Hampton, and Santa Barbara landscape architect Phillip Shipley.

The long drive from the highway shows a great deference to the natural land-scape. None of the "plant a row of plane trees on each side, all the way up" for the Hudsons. When they added shade along the way, they chose native California live oak and black walnut, and they left large areas untouched, to allow enjoyment of the intrinsic beauty of the hills, grass, and scrub oak.

The transition from the wild areas to the domicile is through a shady avenue of ancient, very tall olive trees, along with some hundred-year-old oaks that Lee moved from another area on the property. Becky greets me in the bright, sunny, rather formal courtyard edged with a double row of sycamores.

"Come into the east courtyard, our outdoor living room," she says. "We planted the *Laurus nobilis* hedges to enclose this area, protect it from the wind, and provide a dark green background for the plants."

I follow under the hedge arch into a glorious planting of contrasts—sharp spiny plants against round, soft ones; gray greens against dark greens and char-treuse; oranges against lavenders.

I was curious about the palette chosen for this garden. Becky's answer sur-prised me. She began talking about the *textures.* I had never thought of texture as a palette, but of course, it can be. And it is, in fact, more the texture than anything

The Hudsons' pétanque *court provides a perfect atmosphere for quiet conversation or for casual entertaining with family or friends. Recreational areas have been thoughtfully placed contiguously on the*

west side of the house. Surrounding the pétanque *court is a children's Jungle Gym lawn, an enclosed badminton court, and the pool area, complete with an outdoor kitchen.*

On the sunny west side, Becky created this compelling shade path where white crape myrtle was chosen for the form of its branches and the color of its bark. Marguerite daisies, Yucca filamentosa, variegated myrtles, Clematis montana, Italian cypress, and a Laurus nobilis *hedge mix to exhibit the color and texture treatment so distinctive to this garden. The Lutyens steps are a masterful detail.*

else that gives this garden its quality of excitement. The combinations of large and small, sharp and smooth—dramatic plants like the yucca and flax against the large round flower heads of the *Euphorbia characias wulfenii*—make it extremely vital. A perfect softening effect from pale pink roses scaling trellises and arbors keeps the garden in balance and adds friendliness to the exuberance of the other plants.

"I didn't want fussy plants," Becky says. "Within this formality I wanted a kind of casualness. I wanted that contrast of formality with informal plantings—a garden we could let get ruffled, messed up, kicked around. But there is a difficulty in that, if you let it get too kicked around, then that's exactly what it looks like. We had to have enough structure and yet a relaxed feeling." This they accomplished with patterns of flowers and dark greens forming loose geometric designs around a circular pool.

"Ouch," I say, as I walk past one of the unfussy plants. "Oh," Becky responds, "that's just the *Yucca filamentosa.* It means well! Gertrude Jekyll loved that plant and so do I. Of course, growing up in the desert of Arizona you naturally love yuccas and all the other wild desert things."

That desert upbringing, Becky says, shaped her aesthetic. In conjunction with the texturals, Becky's personal color palette really sets this garden apart from others. The warm colors of Southwest sunsets—hot pink, apricot, coral, brick, gold, and lavender—are seen throughout the Hudson garden. "I've been using these colors over and over—green, orange, yellow, and red. I think people have colors in their subconscious."

Becky's red is what others might call "brick." It appears at the vineyard headquarters on one of the buildings, with windows trimmed in a deep rose. There's a burnt mustard color on another building—very handsome! These are daring colors that command attention; they're exciting, they look right.

In the outdoor dining area, color is not confined to the plants. Becky's wicker furniture is painted a deep ochre, with a dark salmon border. And the pillows on the furniture are raspberry, salmon, and lavender.

Other areas of the garden are equally beautiful, each with a totally different character and purpose: a dramatic viewing terrace with large cactus pots, a children's jungle gym area under the oaks, the quiet, shady west park for meditation or *pétanque,* the recreational pool area in vibrant colors, the citrus walk, and the stately entrance court.

The Hudson garden expresses energy as well as purpose. Having both Lee and Becky interested in gardening accounts for the wide variety and richness here, and gives it an aliveness that only happens when a garden is loved and in constant use. ❦

PREVIOUS PAGES: *The Hudsons*
have achieved a casual splendor
in the east courtyard, their "out-
door living room." Surrounding
arbors support flowering canopies
of pink and white 'Cecile Brunner'
roses and Clematis montana.

THIS PAGE: *Handsome stone*
columns and rose-clad lodge-poles
create a charming dining area.
Around the pool, herbs fill in
between oversized paving stones,
while transplanted olive trees blend
with the surrounding native oaks.

Overview, east courtyard—rich in textures and patterns. Few flowers bloom at this time of the year except for the arbor roses, yet the garden teems with life. ABOVE: *The "garden" of Lee Hudson, esteemed Napa Valley viticulturist.* BELOW: *At ground level, we see the importance of yellow-green variegated myrtle juxtaposed with the gray blue-green euphorbia. The color of the terra-cotta pots, too, contrasts nicely.*

THIS PAGE: *Aerial view and details of the Fisher property. Like grass bending in the wind, the graceful trunks of* Arbutus menziesii *surround the hilltop château.*

OPPOSITE: *The lath house is united with the stone garden houses physically by a pergola and visually by mimicking their shape.* FOLLOWING PAGES: *The unique double lath house covers a glasshouse and provides more filtered light. Alternating gray and green* Santolina *create a stunning pattern.*

ANNIE FISHER HAS SOME SAGE ADVICE TO OFFER ANYONE planning to landscape a large piece of property: "Take your dream plan and then simplify!"

When she and her late husband Pieter began planning their garden at Clos de la Montagne, for example, she envisioned a runnel cutting across a large expanse of lawn, feeling the sound of water would enliven the setting. "But Pieter said, 'That's too elaborate. Let's get rid of it,'" Annie recalls, "and that simplification made the garden much more serene."

The couple put a lifetime of ideas into the creation of their magnificent French château and garden perched on a wooded forty-acre knoll overlooking the Napa Valley. Transforming the ideas that they had gathered from magazines and travels into reality was no simple task.

When they joined forces with Berkeley landscape architect Mai Arbegast, creative sparks flew: "Pieter flipped over Mai," Annie recalls. "She said, 'Tell me what you want and I'll make it for you,' and she did, making our ideas work within the topography of a California setting."

And a spectacular setting it is, with a forest coming right up to the edge of the formal gardens. A logical move might have been for the owners to clear away the trees, which block the view of the valley from the house, but they chose instead to groom the surrounding forest for good health, and let the views of the valley unfold for those who walked the property. "Pieter always had a good sense of topography," Annie acknowledges, "and we really didn't want to see everything at once."

The design of the garden was left largely in Pieter's hands while Annie tackled the complex task of supervising the completion of their home. Borrowing from the tradition of a ha-ha (a ditch, out of sight, that originally was designed as an invisible fence to keep animals out), Pieter ingeniously had the pool recessed in the lawn, so that it wouldn't distract from the view of the Mayacamas mountain range. It was also his idea to establish a *potager* for fresh vegetables, to build matching greenhouses and high-ceilinged lath houses side by side, and the list goes on.

When Arbegast accepts a client, she routinely provides them with Marina Schinz's beautiful *Visions of Paradise,* asking them to mark the pages with ideas they might like to see played out in their gardens.

Architectural integrity is evident everywhere, from the turrets to the garden structures. Flesh-toned buildings are emphasized by peach and lavender pansy window boxes. In the heart-shaped section of the parterre, reddish orange pansies contrast with gray Cerastium tomentosum.

OPPOSITE: *Here, recreational areas become garden features. On the tennis court fence climbing 'Blaze', 'White Dawn', and 'New Dawn' roses take over. The pool— on a lower level, not visible from the house—becomes an axis point for a new garden.*

This arbor setting could be a Californian rendition of a Monet painting. The curve of the arch repeats in the circular lawn rose area and embraces the panoramic view of the Napa Valley and the Mayacamas Mountains beyond. Bursts of red penstemon, 'Firebird', accent the path while climbing roses fight for space with the prolific potato vine, Solanum jasminoides.

And so it was with the Fishers, whose extensive travels had already provided plenty of inspiration for their plans.

Planning for the project was monumental, according to Arbegast, and the gardens took three years to complete. "Pieter wanted a lot of flowering trees, and we were able to bring in some unusual magnolias and flowering cherries. And then we planted olives and citrus around the terrace, since that was the hottest place. I also wanted to be sure something with fragrance would be in bloom throughout the year."

When you add to this assortment of plants the shadeland area of oakleaf hydrangeas, azaleas, rhododendrons, and violets, plus the native madrones, manzanitas, oaks, toyons, and big leaf maples, you have the woodsy feeling of a garden that's been established for twenty years. Amazingly, the garden was just completed four years ago, at the same time the château was ready for occupancy.

Joining Mai Arbegast in the planting of the terraced flower beds was noted Bay Area landscaper Sarah Hammond, who added a handsome textural combination of Mediterranean plants—*Plecostachys,* lavenders, rosemary, euphorbia, erigeron, santolina, and a tiny, cloud-like white aster.

"This is a California garden," Arbegast observes, "which has a Mediterranean look combined with the images of French, English, and Italian flower borders, all worked into a cohesive whole to provide a sense of serenity."

The energy and joy that Pieter gave to constructing this garden goes on today, in spite of his passing. A testimony to his courage battling cancer was his determination to see his dream garden become a reality; he wouldn't let go until it had been completed. ❦

Every year more than ten thousand tulips ordered from Holland parade across the landscape of Al and DeDe Wilsey. This spectacular

show lasts about a month. OPPOSITE: *The view from the terrace encompasses the vast sweep of tulips edging the entire garden.*

ABOVE: *A more casual mix of colors and varieties is planted on the street side of the property for visitors and photographers to enjoy.*

ALTHOUGH DEDE WILSEY LOVES HER SEVERAL GARDENS IN THE NAPA VALLEY AND TAKES THE lead in their development, she does not masquerade as a "true" gardener who revels in the arts of composting and double-digging.

"My mother had a beautiful three-acre garden at her home in Washington, D.C.," DeDe recalls. "One day we were talking and I said I was sad that I'd never inherited the gardening genes that made her want to dig in the earth. And she said, *'Dig?* When have you ever seen me dig?' And it was a sudden revelation: you can have fun gardening without ever getting your hands dirty!"

Laughing at the recollection, DeDe says she then bought dozens of garden books and magazines and, on cold winter days, would sit by the fireplace with a huge handmade map she'd drawn of the garden, making crayon drawings and pasting pictures where she wanted the garden to come to life.

And that's how she gardens at the weekend home she shares with her husband Al. "I really enjoy putting together gardens," she enthuses, "so for the past few years, I've been finding little places that need fixing up, so that I can design the gardens, too."

We set out on a walking tour of her home's spacious grounds and were immediately greeted by the awesome sight of thirty-nine thousand brand-new tulips in long drifts of strong pink and pale, creamy yellow, blooming in all their glory. Ironically, the seasonal demands of her husband's business and her own career as chair of the Fine Arts Museums of San Francisco usually keep them at their San Francisco residence during the peak of tulip time.

One March when the Wilseys cleared their weekend schedules to be on hand for the bulbous color show, the Napa River so flooded the property that a neighbor came to visit on his Jet Ski. Suddenly DeDe found herself with a huge landscape that needed redoing. Enlisting the eager assistance of her head gardener Michael Cadigan, she met the challenge.

And with the enthusiasm of a child rushing to open presents on Christmas morning, she continues to improve and update. "I just can't wait to get up here on the weekends," DeDe confesses, "It's not an elaborate garden or terribly imaginative—I just want to be able to stand anywhere on this property and see flowers that look like they're already arranged in a container."

Although a number of landscapers have worked on the garden in the past, it was the late Leland Noel's graceful structural layout and his selective choice and placement of trees that carry the elegance of the garden through the seasons, even without bedding plants.

When we return to the porch, Al is there with their six dogs, waiting for a report on what we've seen and, most importantly, what new plans DeDe has in mind.

"Al," DeDe smiles, "enjoys the beauty of this place as much as I do." ❦

The quiet grandeur of the Wilsey garden is interrupted only by seasonal changes in floral and foliage displays. In summer, brilliant pink petunias replace the bulbs, and pink crape myrtle repeats the color overhead. The horse pasture is visible across the creek past the irregularly shaped pond. OPPOSITE: *Setting the* Liquidambars *and white oleanders back from the road creates a gracious entrance.*

HARMONY OF CULTURES

SOMETIMES MORE THAN ONE COUNTRY HAS A CALLING FOR US, AND

WE ARE HAPPIEST WITH A COMBINATION OF CULTURES. PETER AND SU

HUA NEWTON MASTERFULLY BLEND ENGLISH AND CHINESE INTER-

ESTS; MARIA MANETTI FARROW COMBINES HER NEW AMERICAN HOME-

LAND WITH HER NATIVE TUSCAN; THE WILSONS HAVE BROUGHT

SOUTH AFRICAN ELEMENTS AND MORE TO THE NAPA VALLEY,

PREVIOUS PAGES: *View from Maria Farrow's terrace.* ABOVE: *The sculptural bridge leads from the parking area over the pool to the garden. At the entrance gate, plantings of tall cypress and olive introduce a taste of Tuscany.* BELOW: *Gracing copper trellises against the honey-colored house is the 'Coral Dawn' rose.*

IN MAY, WHEN DICK AND I VISITED THE HOME OF MARIA Manetti Farrow, it was like stepping into another world.

Over the sound of gravel crunching under the tires as we entered the parking area, we heard the faint sound of music. Alert and curious, we entered the garden through an arbor cloaked in sweet-smelling *Jasminum polyanthum* and purple wisteria and were enveloped in the aria, "Un Bel Di" from Puccini's *Madame Butterfly.* Its intensity seemed to neither wax nor wane as we ascended the ten-foot-wide bridge that arches over a giant swimming pool the way bridges span canals in Venice.

Directly ahead, across a broad manicured sweep of lawn punctuated by two enormous oaks, lay a long, low Tuscan villa with a red tile roof and walls a pale eggshell tone of yellow.

In moments, Maria arrives, her greeting heavily flavored with the melodic sound of her homeland. "I am Florentine," she says, "and until twenty years ago lived in Tuscany. For me, the hills between Florence and Tuscany, with their grapes, cypresses, and olive trees, are among the most beautiful places in the world, and I consider the Napa Valley an American paradise countryside."

She leads a slow-paced tour around the exterior of her home, situated on an eight-foot berm that gives it proper elevation above the valley floor,

explaining its genesis: "In 1985, this place was all flat, with a horse corral. And the house that was here before I didn't like, so I tore it down."

"The garden is very simple, very linear, like the house," she explains. And, like the major gardens in her native Italy, the plant palette is a simple one. But each planting is significant. There are about a hundred oleanders, for example. Many are the white-flowered 'Sister Agnes' variety that drops its blossoms when they are spent.

A harmonious scheme unites the planting of some five hundred to six hundred rose bushes; they are arranged in color blocks of twelve to twenty-four plants each. The roses supply a large quantity of cut flowers for this home and Maria's apartment in San Francisco.

She stops from time to time, naming a rose and asking, "Do you know this one?" She strokes its foliage the way a doting mother would pat the heads of her children. "There aren't too many colors because I concentrate on the colors that I love."

Inside the lattice-fenced rose garden, the plants are bordered by *Iberis sempervirens* and bearded irises—yellow, white, apricot on the sides, and lavender and blue at the end. A similar lattice-fenced area on the other shoulder of the house encloses a large vegetable garden, which supplies Maria's kitchen.

"I love flowers," she says, "and eventually want to spend more time working in the garden, to under-

A one-inch-square gray lattice is a perfect frame for pinkish-white Jasminum polyanthum *against purple wisteria. While the fish fountain gives a focal point to the rose garden, the strength of this area is in the harmonious selection of colors—lavender, pink, and gold irises at the base—blending with pink roses, such as 'Inspiration'. The olympic-sized pool seems in perfect scale to the magnificent trees and grounds.*

LEFT: *Silvery olive and dark cypress, a traditional combination in Italy, surround the garden on five-foot mounds, covered with vinca and low-growing junipers. Additional plantings of pale pink and white oleanders—kept smaller than the olives—add a cool note in late summer. Flanking each side of the Tuscan villa is a lattice courtyard. This one encloses roses and irises; the other, herbs and vegetables. The giant ancient valley oaks seem to dwarf the rose court and even the tall cypress. THIS PAGE: Large lotus-shaped cement urns on pillars are repeated around the terrace. The urns, filled only with rosemary, lend a soft elegance to the formal rhythm. Across the spacious lawn, irises planted in waves of color backed with roses make a gentle transition to the geometric rows of grapevines beyond. RIGHT: Maria embraces Gioia.*

stand even more about it. I love the statement of simplicity. For ten years I've worked every weekend with my gardening consultant, Jean Michels, a delightful lady who helped lay out parts of the garden and understands microclimates here in the Valley."

But keeping everything maintained to Maria's standards is no easy task, especially when she spends her work week in San Francisco, so she has devised a unique method of detailed recordkeeping. An oversized loose-leaf folder holds computerized spreadsheets on which the garden is divided into sixteen separate sections. On the computer printout for each section is a description of the area, its irrigation needs, a year-round fertilization program, and complete day-to-day care.

"You know, among the fruit orchard, the flower beds, and the vegetable garden, it's about sixteen acres of landscape," Maria says, rolling her eyes. "It's so much work, even for three gardeners. So I leave a schedule for them every week. And with these computer printouts, when I'm talking with them we're all talking the same language. For every month I have a calendar for what flowers are in bloom."

And is it worth all that work?

"Ah," she smiles, "I come here Friday, Saturday, and Sunday and get a big lift. And no headaches!" ☙

Stella Wilson, a marvelous cook, loves to entertain on this inviting terrace overlooking the entire Napa Valley. Breaking up the long curve of balustrade and rock wall are pots of flowering pink and white pelargoniums. A bulb-lined path leads around the house to another outdoor living space on the west side, looking toward the Vaca Mountains.

The handsome Chimney Rock Winery, owned by Hack and Stella Wilson, was built in the same Cape Dutch architectural style as their home. Bright primary-

colored flowers, such as the red, yellow, and blue primulas and hot pink geraniums found in her garden, express Stella's energetic personality. A rose-covered arch

leads through extensive herb and vegetable gardens, all grown from seed, including the peach tree flowering in the background.

OFTENTIMES, STELLA WILSON REFERS TO HER TWELVE-YEAR-OLD HOME AND GARDEN AS A League of Nations project. She is South African, her husband Hack is American, their architect is Austrian-German, their interior decorator is Chinese, and their gardener Manuel is Hispanic.

Their white stucco home reflects the Cape Dutch architecture of her native South Africa, and Stella went to great lengths to surround it with plants that flourish there. Calla lilies (which grow in such profusion on the Cape that they are sometimes disdainfully referred to as pig lilies), birds of paradise, gerbera daisies, pelargoniums, lilies-of-the-Nile, and summer bulbs bloom by the score. "South Africa has more native flora than any other country in the world," she says. Fields and fields of gerbera (in Africa, Namaqualand) daisies cover the Cape Mountains.

Stella also grows South African vegetables and fruits that she can't buy here. "We start them in our new greenhouse," she says. "Limestone lettuce and gem squash are two of my favorites. The squash is green when it's ready to eat, then turns yellow in winter and it's still good. The fruit orchard has some interesting varieties too: incredible red peaches, another peach that's dark yellow and hard—it never gets soft, so it makes a great canning peach. Manuel and I save the pits to plant new trees. He's marvelous; he never throws anything away."

She makes good use of all these fruits and vegetables, as she is a superb cook and loves to entertain. Undaunted by large groups, Stella does all the cooking for as many as a hundred guests. In addition to a great kitchen and dining room, two outdoor living areas work well for large-scale entertaining. The east terrace, filled with potted plants, catches the morning sun and looks back to the hills. The larger terrace on the other side of the house has the afternoon sun and a view of the entire Napa Valley.

From each frequent visit to her homeland, Stella brings back a remembrance: a lily the South Africans call "chincherinchee." "It's like a tuberose, but with a much heavier head, and it has an overpowering fragrance!"

Everywhere in the garden, Stella has put her mark. Bright color combinations express her joy: deep purple blue against red here, red and yellow there. There's an approachability to this garden—a friendliness. It wasn't enough for Stella to have a beautiful curved stone rock wall on the drive up; in a gesture of welcoming, she topped it with terra-cotta pots of geraniums.

Does her husband also share her enthusiasm for gardening? "Hack doesn't know the first thing about it," she laughs, "but he likes the looks of what I'm doing and he's very diplomatic about constructive criticism."

Diplomacy is always important in a League of Nations. ❦

Purple Salvia nemorosa *'East*

Friesland' is contained in a double

boxwood hedge. BELOW: *'Golden*

Desert' ash (Fraxinus oxycarpa)

lines the drive to the house. Beneath

the ash, flowering Mazus reptans

'Albus' lies flat. OPPOSITE:

Frozen in bronze, a pair of cranes

preen before this incredible screen

of Cedrus atlantica *'Glauca*

Pendula', designed and pruned

by Peter Newton.

"TOO MUCH VIEW. NOT A BLADE OF GRASS LEFT. A SPARTAN five-acre site."

Anyone looking at the magnificent gardens of Su Hua and Peter Newton today would find this description by Peter hard to believe.

The land in the Mayacamas mountain range was purchased in 1978 for a hillside vineyard and a new winery, after Peter sold Sterling Vineyards. (He had concluded that the grapes from Sterling's hillside vineyards produced the best wine.) On his new property, only about 20 percent of the 560 wooded acres proved plantable. The rest was too mountainous.

The herculean task of clearing rocks and carving terraces for the planting of vines on the steep slopes soon began. After most of the vineyard was in, Peter turned his attention to the garden. It's fascinating to learn how he conceived this enormous project: "The site began as the creation of the bulldozer—a brutal starting point. We were left with no vegetation. All the topsoil had to be imported. A bare-bones master plan was prepared for the irrigation, the structure of the terraces, and the theme of each of the gardens."

As Peter started to sketch out the plans for the garden, he realized much of it would have to be terraced boldly, imaginatively, and that it would need to be integrated into the landscape. The dramatic long terraces of purple wisteria in the garden today, which seem like an extension of the vineyard on the hillside below the house, illustrate how successful he was.

Another of Peter's major concerns was—of all things—the view! Across the Valley, on our hill, I consider the view our greatest asset, and it was difficult for me to comprehend that a view could be a detriment. This is how Peter explained it: "The panoramic view has been a source of abiding concern. To gain intimacy, gardens need to be enclosed spaces, like rooms leading from one to another. It is a major distraction if one's eyes are drawn constantly to some spectacle in the distance—even if that happens to be the whole glorious Napa Valley. The need to eliminate, or at least to contain, the view, has therefore been a preoccupation."

The result, this audacious and multifaceted garden, is extraordinary in many ways: first, because of the scale—it's really a dozen gardens in one (none of them small), and each one a surprise, totally different from the other; second, because the owner, who is not a professional landscape architect, designed them himself (with one exception—the

Asian garden). Besides the imaginative designs of the various gardens, the variety of plant material is staggering. As a mountain dweller myself, I was astounded by the many solutions Peter found to cover the stark slopes of different exposures. He said planting ground covers was the first step in taming the site after the bulldozers had gone.

One of the most impressive is the low-growing miniature white rose ('Gourmet Popcorn'), which is simply sheared off after blooms have faded. The repeating blooms make it a great choice for constant beauty. I was impressed with a prostrate *Cotoneaster* closely hugging the almost vertical slope. A flat rosemary and *Arctostaphylos uva-ursi* are also used on the steepest slopes. An unusual planting of white clover has a soft inviting effect below the wisteria and continues on to the lion entrance. Just inside the gate a planting of *Mazus reptans* 'Albus' makes a neat yellow green carpet below rows of golden ash. Peter's use of gardenias, heathers, and crape myrtle on different hillsides is unexpected and very successful. Oh yes, then there's the beautiful chartreuse Scotch moss and dark green, lavender-flowering thyme used in the Zen garden. Each of the ground covers has been selected not only for its erosion-controlling property but also for the color, texture, and particular sun exposure in that location.

To better understand the creative ingenuity reflected in the Newton property, let's look into a few of Peter's garden rooms. To me, the parterre that roofs the Newton Winery is perhaps the most original and beautiful treatment of a winery anywhere in the world. "Besides," Peter smiles, "it's a great way to keep the wines cool while aging."

But as we approach the parterre, even before it comes into view, the rows of dark green juniper topiaries arrest our attention. *Juniperus chinensis* 'Spartan' trimmed in a corkscrew shape add a sense of whimsy and drama. Then we climb a short staircase and are startled by the beautiful and complex scene of neatly clipped box hedges forming diamond patterns containing white 'Popcorn' roses on the perimeter, lavender *Nepeta*, dark green *Teucrium*, and gray santolina on the interior squares. A bubbling fountain adds life and focus to the center of the parterre. At the far end are fourteen varieties of lavender in shades from dark purple to white.

With its strong geometric patterns and backdrops of tall, dark green cypress, the garden totally domi-

PREVIOUS PAGES: *Winery roof parterre encloses miniature floribunda roses, santolina, germander, and 'Gourmet Popcorn' roses.*

THIS PAGE: *British lions in a bed of prostrate clover ('Kent Wild White') guard the Chinese gate, richly curtained by* Thuja occidentalis *'Smaragd.' Standard roses of 'French Lace' at two different heights enclose the predominantly white rose garden accented with pale yellow and apricot.*

BELOW: *Aerial view from a balloon of the rose garden and weeping garden.*

Inspired by a tea house in China, the Newtons created their conical thatched-roof tea house on the edge of the croquet lawn that dips over the horizon into rows of colonnaded wisteria vines. The vertical lines of the golden cypress (Cupressus sempervirens *'Swane's Golden'*) *draw our eye across the vast lawn and lead it up to the horizontal rose trellises.*

nates the area. Buildings, appropriately camouflaged with brown lattice, appear more like greenhouses than office buildings and wine laboratories.

Leaving the winery we pass through a dramatic Chinese red gate that startles, then reminds us of the blending of two cultures in the Newton gardens. On the road toward the house and the rest of the gardens, we encounter the awesome view Peter has so well controlled in the garden areas. Seeing the steep slopes and rocky, thin soils of the surrounding terraced vineyards only makes his garden all the more amazing.

Several gardens lead up to the house. The most impressive for me is the weeping garden. The term *weeping* has nothing to do with sadness, but describes the trailing habits of this area's plantings. The steps are interlaced with a weeping form of *Cotoneaster adpressus.* There are double-flowered weeping cherry trees around the perimeter, and an extraordinary eight-foot-tall, sixty-foot-long curtain of weeping blue atlas cedar, *Cedrus atlantica* 'Glauca Pendula,' forms a backdrop for the boxwood parterres containing brilliant purple *Salvia nemorosa* 'East Friesland.' Equally as compelling as the brilliant color contrast of purple and light green is the unusual shape of the parterre and surrounding convex curves of broader box hedges containing the cherry trees. Also unique are the two-layer box hedges edging the salvia—the lower one only four inches high and fourteen inches wide, giving greater breadth to the walkway.

Up another set of stone steps, this time softened with creeping fig (*Ficus pumila*), is the formal rose garden. Hundreds of white, yellow, and apricot roses are laid out in curved beds divided by grass paths.

Peter leads the way under the wooden arch into the Zen garden, explaining, "The transition is abrupt. The western world is left behind. Here, in a dry Zen garden, the sea is represented by half an acre of crushed granite, raked in ever-varying patterns. In its midst are set, with the usual Chinese care, groupings of rocks that were found during the course of all that bulldozing. No color is used," Peter continues, "for tranquillity and mood are what the garden is all about. This garden has one vital credential, a Chinese designer—my wife, Su Hua. I am convinced that no western person, however studious, can capture the essence of an Asian garden."

We have come through a series of garden rooms and our eyes welcome the spacious green croquet lawn with a thatched tea house in the upper right corner. Across the lawn, a long, graceful perennial border is in bloom in soft tones of gray, lavender, white, and dark green, accentuated by spots of yellow. There is a delightful, gentle rhythm to the border, powerfully set off by tall dark cypresses. An important structural element of this perennial border is that it is planted on a slope; you not only see more of it, but it leads your eye up the hill to the trellised rose garden.

Beyond the croquet lawn, through the pool-pond area, is my favorite part of the garden. Another vertical garden, this time all green—yellow green, blue green, emerald green—probably at least seventeen different shades of green and all in conifers.

I wonder out loud if Peter had it in mind to create a garden of this stature when he started here. He grew up in a world of gardens; his mother was one of those great English amateur gardeners who tended plants as if they were her children. "Gardening is in my soul," Peter replies.

Quiet moments. Toadstool seats in woods. So much richness in this garden, often surprises—certainly a horticultural delight. There's so much to learn about design, patterns, and unusual plant materials. If anything, there is too much for one visit. We need to be on our best behavior, so we will be invited back. ❦

OPPOSITE: *Punctuating the rich tapestry of conifers are autumn colors of the beautiful* Cryptomeria japonica *'Elegans' and Japanese maple. Steps at the pool provide the architectural device for an unusual waterfall.* LEFT: *Climbing orangish 'Piñata' drops pinkish petals, creating a pathway befitting a queen.*

The moment you enter the Asian garden, you slow down and perhaps speak a little softer. It's amazing what a calming effect such simple elements as stone, sand, and a few evergreens can have. OPPOSITE: The stones used in the Zen garden came from vineyard clearing. The quiet rhythm changes with each new raking, but always the result is one of serenity. THIS PAGE: Red Chinese gates sing a joyous note against the rich green backdrop. A tall, delicately balanced sculpture near the entrance provides an almost human welcome in stone. Side by side, two cultures, two paths cross the sand.

GIFTS FROM THE GOLDEN STATE

GARDENS OF THE NAPA VALLEY HAVE A LOOK OF THEIR OWN, PAR-

TIALLY BECAUSE THEY ARE BACKDROPPED BY VINEYARDS AND MOUN-

TAINS. THE GARDENS PRESENTED IN THIS CHAPTER USE ADDITIONAL

FEATURES THAT ARE DISTINCTIVE TO THIS MEDITERRANEAN CLIMATE,

SUCH AS ROCKY HILLSIDES, AN OLD VINEYARD RESERVOIR, OR PAR-

TICULAR PLANTS ADAPTABLE TO OUR DRY, HOT SUMMERS.

PREVIOUS PAGES: *Araujo stair-*

way. THIS PAGE: *Rising abruptly*

from flat vineyards, the hillside gar-

den of Bill Hewitt pays testimony to

his love of California native plants.

Poppies are kept blooming with reg-

ular irrigation. The first time Bill

saw this property it was filled with

wildflowers. He continues to recreate

that gentle, natural landscape.

The solid rock walls of the home

designed by Kevin Roche are soft-

ened in appearance by more native

plants and grasses. A closer look

into the trellised courtyard reveals a

handsome planting of natives:

ceanothus 'Dark Star', prostrate

Baccharis, and the low-growing

Arctostaphylos 'Emerald

Carpet'. Even in our summer heat

this manzanita stays bright green.

WHEN BILL HEWITT AND HIS LATE WIFE PURCHASED SIXTY-nine acres of vineyards in the Napa Valley in 1960, they immediately recognized a rocky knoll in the middle of the vineyards as an ideal site for a home. At the time, the only structure atop the hill was a large redwood water tank.

In 1990, they built La Villette (French for "the village") and decided to do the landscape entirely in native plants. No lawns anywhere. The only hint of a "traditional" garden is the forty tree roses planted in a row along the outside of the driveway that encircles the base of the knoll.

The twelve-thousand-square-foot home, designed by famed architect Kevin Roche, seems almost to have grown up among the native madrones and oaks on the hilltop, and its large windows afford stunning views in every direction.

Napa Valley landscape architect Steve Arns was contracted to lay out the garden, softening the angular lines of the walls of Napa Valley rubble-stone with a distinctive palette of native shrubs and bunch grasses intermixed with bulbs like crocus and daffodil and an assortment of Mediterranean plants. The color is particularly impressive in spring, as California poppies open their flowers to the sun, ceanothus blooms in a deep purple that dazzles the eyes, and California redbud trees show off their ruby branches against the blue sky. Oaks, too, seem to

glow at sunset when the light catches their yellow catkins. Monkeyflowers, manzanita, *Calycanthus occidentalis*, verbena, oleander, and penstemon put on a seasonal show, along with salvias, white dogwood, olive trees, and blue-flowered rosemary, which tumbles down the hillside.

"The first time we saw this hill, it was a mound of golden poppies," Hewitt, a former ambassador to Jamaica, recalls. Under the direction of landscape architect Jonathan Plant, the hillside was hydroseeded with poppies to help restore that glory.

At the base of the hill is a fruit orchard that includes apple, plum, pear, peach, persimmon, fig, orange, and lemon trees. Inside the courtyard, *Hardenbergia* softens the trellis with its dark green leaves and deep purple blossoms in the winter, and in summer, star jasmine cools the area with its white flowers and light perfume. Adding a light green, beautiful leaf to the overhead summer shade is, of course, the best plant of all—the grapevine. Hewitt says, "I wanted to give my guests a close-up view of the grapes and the distinctive leaf shapes." 🍇

The Cafferatas' lovely barn and former temporary residence focuses upon their man-made yet natural-looking lake rimmed by weeping willows, huge swaths of oenothera, verbena, and golden coreopsis, and patrolled by a very possessive Mr. Swan. The masterful grouping of plants and trees around the lake create a bucolic setting and wildlife habitat. LOWER LEFT: *Floribunda 'Betty Prior' blooms continuously at the edge of the raised beds.*

OFF THE SILVERADO TRAIL A FEW HUNDRED FEET IS A good-looking redwood barn. For the last several years Janie and Frank Cafferata have had their offices and their temporary home in this handsome structure, while their house was being completed. During that time they created the most marvelous lake garden, by turning two problems—heavy clay soil and an empty, abandoned reservoir—into assets.

When the Cafferatas decided to fill the lake, they wanted to enlarge it and sculpt its shape. Ingeniously, they agreed to trade the excess mountains of clay to a contractor for Sterling Winery in exchange for the excavation. Although it took over a year to remove the clay, one truckload at a time, they finally have accomplished their goal and also provided the perfect material for the lining of Sterling's reservoir.

When I noted how clean and natural the pond looked, Janie replied, "There was some trial and error, but the fishery people guided us to the right combinations of plants and fish—bottom-dwelling catfish were used, along with bluegill and large-mouth bass, to control the bluegill population." They seem to have found the right balance, as the pond is clear and beautiful.

Purple 'Voodoo Magic' irises from Louisiana grow along the edge. Sweeping plantings of Mexican primrose (*Oenothera*), spots of purple verbena, and sprinkles of golden daisies define the path around the lake, punctuated by clumps of yellow irises given to the Cafferatas by Mel Juler, gardener at Château Montelena Winery.

Janie's selections and groupings of plants and trees surrounding the pool are masterful. The rhythm of the carefully placed weeping willow, birch, and poplar trees keeps the eye moving gently up, around, and finally into the lake, which outlines their peaceful reflections.

An acre pond—quite an amazing undertaking for a novice. Gardening with her mother from the time she was a child has given Janie confidence as well as knowledge.

The lake is now a special habitat where hummingbirds, butterflies, frogs, and fish play happily. Blue heron and wild ducks try to visit, but Mr. Swan at present thinks he owns the pond. The Cafferatas are in the process of trying to find him a mate and to import some geese to make a more democratic society. 🦢

Determined to maintain and expand upon the natural beauty of their canyon homesite, the owners of this property were assisted by landscape architect Jack Chandler in extending nature right up to their front door. Painstaking plant selection included as many "deerproof" species as possible, such as cistus, daphne, rosemary, ceanothus, manzanita, and santolina. OPPOSITE: Jack Chandler gives us a marvelous example of how a swimming pool can become a reflecting pond. The surrounding plantings are native. Trees are left to arch over for shade; boulders are used for diving rocks. Napa Valley architect Ray Rector designed this unusual home in sculptural forms to fit into the hillside with natural planting and a deep pink rockrose for color.

STUNNINGLY BEAUTIFUL ASPECTS OF THE NAPA VALLEY, OFTEN OVERLOOKED BY VISITORS who confine their travel to the valley floor, are found on the wild mountainsides where deep ravines provide a growing ground for native oaks, manzanitas, and madrones and a habitat for deer and other wildlife. Often, too, this beauty is obliterated by homes and gardens with lawns, flower beds, and precise foundation plantings better suited for suburban development.

But the owners of at least one mountainside home were determined that their dwelling would nestle into its setting as if it had always been there. After purchasing nearly two hundred acres of land to ensure their privacy, they selected Napa architect Ray Rector to design a pure Napa Valley home and engaged landscape architect Jack Chandler to preserve and enhance the native environment.

"It's a difficult site," Chandler says, "and we had to put up with deer the first four years, until the owners put up five thousand running feet of fence." The main entry to the house was from the garage, but Chandler designed a new approach from a gravel parking area. Concrete steps angle back and forth through boulders and olive trees complementing the adobe brick home with its large curved windows.

"We brought in these olive trees," Chandler says, "along with mayten trees, which are doing remarkably well in containers. We used rockrose, coffeeberry, manzanita, *Teucrium*, *Elaeagnus ebbingei*, 'Julia Phelps' ceanothus, and as many other drought-tolerant and deerproof plants as we could. But deerproof elsewhere is somebody else's salad here—all deer don't eat the same things."

Both the plantings and the pool feel as though nature herself had been the designer. The pool, irregularly shaped and dark bottomed, has native stone coping and a diving rock for a diving board.

The owners added their own aspect to the landscape with a vegetable garden in which mother and son began planting citrus and other fruit trees and built a series of grow boxes on the steep hillside behind the house. The citrus, rosemary,

and lavender attract hundreds of butterflys to the one-third-acre hillside garden.

In early spring, leeks, cabbage, garlic, and onions are in full production. Summer standouts include melons from France and Israel, along with squash, corn, tomatoes, and sunflowers. Numerous artichokes produce enough fruit on the sunny hillside that the owners deliberately allow many to pass maturity and burst into iridescent blue blossoms.

The marriage of the gardening son several years ago put a temporary damper on the vegetable planting fervor, but now "grandma" has been joined on her hillside by an equally enthusiastic granddaughter, and the garden is in full production again. ❦

The Cliff May design of Robert and

Margrit Mondavi's home on an his-

toric and archeologically significant

site, Wappo Hill, puts few obstacles

between the owners and nature. The

glass wall of the year-round pool

area brings the forest inside, while a

canopy of oak branches defines an

outdoor dining room.

A VISIT TO THE GARDEN OF ROBERT AND MARGRIT MONDAVI almost always includes a short walk from the house to an outlook atop Wappo Hill.

"Just over there," Margrit says, pointing to a spot among large boulders, "was where the Wappo tribe held celebratory ceremonies. And when they were relocated it wasn't long before all four thousand of them died off. Today there's not a single full-blooded Wappo left."

As Dick and I follow the long drive up to the house, it's as if a ribbon of asphalt had been gently unrolled amidst rock outcroppings and native oaks and manzanita, disturbing as little as possible. A planting of white daisies alongside the road is the first signal that the parking area, with its castle-like, fifteen-foot stone retaining wall (topped with a vigorous blue-flowered wisteria vine), is just ahead.

Mounting steps from the gravel parking area, one finds unobtrusive plantings of seasonal color. Just before you reach the front door there is a fragrant planting of star jasmine, a group of sparkling red roses planted against a backdrop of boulders, and a view that goes forever.

Ever the gracious hostess, Margrit leads us outdoors to a small garden area among oak trees, while explaining the purpose of the garden is to give "windows" through the branches of the trees for views of the countryside below.

"When the winery bought five hundred acres here in 1968," Margrit says, "the interest was in the flatlands for vineyards, and they scarcely noticed the hill. But about ten years later when Bob and I were looking for a homesite, we hiked up here and thought it was fabulous."

Cliff May, who designed the Robert Mondavi winery, was called upon to design the house. But May, known for his ranch-style homes, had never done a multilevel design before, and proposed bulldozing the hilltop to make room for a garage. In reverence for the site, that idea was scuttled by Margrit, and eventually May agreed.

Initially, landscaper Bob Royston aided Margrit in establishing a basis for a garden. "We understood each other, and he knew that I didn't want anything formal. I wanted nature to come into the house."

The planting beds rimmed by low rock walls outside the home's lower-level garage are where Margrit has installed a wide variety of plants, ranging from culinary herbs to colorful spires of foxglove and enormous green leaves of rhubarb. "I love making rhubarb pies," she says.

Margrit cherishes the idea of being able to garden. "When I have time, I get into it and forget time and place, but that's very seldom," she says. "My husband's travels take him all over and I think it's more important for me to be with him." ☙

ABOVE: *With deference to sur-rounding oaks, manzanita, and madrone, the Mondavis have judi-ciously pruned only where necessary to allow "windows" for views.*

RIGHT: *The parking area is fronted by a fifteen-foot fieldstone wall topped by wisteria vines. Llamas, a birthday present to Bob, thrive in this setting.* OPPOSITE: *Margrit, seated in a lookout niche atop her home.*

Serenity begins at the gate with the

long avenue of olives. Daphne's

restraint is shown in the absence of

any under-planting—simply a low

wall of single stones provides the

subtle definition between vineyard

and driveway.

I LOVE TO VISIT THE ARAUJO GARDEN, NOT ONLY FOR THE sheer beauty, but also for the sense of order and tranquillity the place communicates. There's a serenity that seems completely effortless, but that in fact has taken great discipline to achieve.

When I asked the owner and creator of the garden, Daphne Araujo, how she accomplished such a pure statement, she answered, "I can't really tell you how I did it, except that I'm always trying to throw the extraneous out and not let a little bit of this or that creep in just because it's a plant I like."

Envying Daphne's self-discipline, I quizzed her further: "How can you give up the flowers you love?" "Oh," she responded, "you just let others have them in their gardens. Or you have a picking garden where it doesn't matter. Then I find that all my little spots of color are in boxes that are pretty well controlled. Whenever I'm hungry for color, I can go and enjoy it, but looking out on this garden, I don't want to see it. If we had a lot of flowers, you wouldn't really see the hills or the trees. We love the spring colors and the fall colors and the play of branches in the winter. That for me is what the garden is all about. I'm not into flowers that much. And it surprises me how much people equate gardens with flowers. I felt compelled to find a way not to let this garden lose the feeling that I first had when I saw this property—which was country. I

wanted to feel relaxed when I drove in. I didn't want to see a riot of color."

Part of that sense of country came from a marvelous old white barn, which inspired the development of the new garden, the winery (a redwood building in the shape of a barn), and other buildings, all creating a rural, handsome compound.

Both Daphne and Bart Araujo so appreciated the barn structure that when it was necessary to reconstruct it, they put it back exactly as it was—lopsided and all. Instead of discarding the old lumber as they added the new redwood siding, they turned the boards over and used the unpainted side to panel the offices.

Daphne, who received a degree in landscape architecture from the University of Arizona, attributes her interest in gardening to two things: to being reared in a military family and seeing so many beautiful, historical places at an early age, and to her grandmother's two-and-one-half acre garden in Maryland. After having lived on the East Coast, in Turkey, and Honolulu, she settled in Santa Barbara, a perfect climate to practice her landscaping.

When they moved to the Napa Valley, she wisely did not try to recreate the lush green, almost tropical gardens of Santa Barbara. Here, she began concentrating on the rural California aspect, clearing the tall hedges in front of the barn so it could be seen as you

drove in. Entering through a tunnel of old olives with vineyards on each side, there is nothing to distract our eye from exactly what Daphne Araujo wants us to see: the rural scene of two redwood barns spaced graciously apart—here and there softened by magnificent stands of grasses. To the right are some small buildings almost hidden by trees, arbors, and vines.

The parking area in front of the first barn and main residence was created by building unmortared rock walls. "A dry wall is a structure without being formalized," Daphne says. "It *cannot* be formalized. It's relaxed. And then it's the same thing with the grasses. We felt they had to be an important part of the garden because they cannot be hedged, they cannot be balled. They just do what they do. The joy we have living here is living with the seasons. The grasses echo that seasonal thrill. Spring is early green, in the summer it's all flowers, in the fall it's the autumn colors, and in the winter they're still full of color in the garden. In late summer, when other plants look wilted, the grasses thrive."

Against large inert areas of gravel, soft, gently waving grasses provide an element of life and friendliness. Their slow rhythmic motion tends to have a calming and cooling effect in the midsummer heat. The many different varieties of grasses are grouped in clumps. One that's particularly appealing is

Mexican feather grass. "It's an irresistible one. You just can't walk by it without skimming the top with your fingers. In the summer we comb it with a hair comb. Their seed heads get so heavy, they get weighted down. It's like grooming a dog," Daphne laughingly explains.

Neat, low-clipped rosemary and the quiet repetition of ancient olives down the drive add to the tranquil feeling here. The needly texture and dark green color of the rosemary play well against the gray green, narrow-leafed olive trees—a classic Mediterranean combination. Originally, there were dark purple plum trees in between the olives, but Daphne felt the alternating purple and silver did not present a relaxing effect. So, true to her personal vision of the whole, she replaced the plums with more olives and created the peaceful, beautiful entrance to her vineyard farm. ❦

BIG LITTLE GARDENS

DRIVING THROUGH THE RESIDENTIAL AREAS CLOSE TO ST. HELENA IN THE

SPRINGTIME, YOU WILL SEE ONE CHARMING GARDEN AFTER ANOTHER. IT

SEEMS EVERYONE HERE LOVES TO GARDEN, ESPECIALLY IN THAT SEASON.

THE SIZE OF THE GARDEN DOESN'T REALLY MATTER; IT'S THE SCOPE OF

IMAGINATION THE GARDENER DEMONSTRATES. IN THIS CHAPTER, WE

LOOK AT LITTLE GARDENS THAT HAVE A BIG EFFECT—ONE GARDEN

EXHIBITS FORMALITY IN A SMALL AREA, ONE USES LARGE URNS AS A GAR-

DEN FEATURE, AND ANOTHER SHOWCASES NATIVE PLANTS AND SHRUBS ON

A HILLSIDE ALONG WITH SOME CLOSELY PLANTED PERENNIALS.

PREVIOUS PAGES: *Blossom time at Fred Lyon's.* ABOVE: *Topsoil ranging from shallow to none was an obstacle for Ray and Jane Garassino, but a soil improvement plan permitted planting flax, artemisia, nepeta, Helichrysum petiolare 'Limelight', red Japanese maple, and ornamental grasses in their entry garden, as well as on a steep hillside above the swimming pool. The garden, though small, contains an arresting combination of plants, and the enthusiasm of an avid gardener.*

STARTING FROM SCRATCH PRETTY MUCH DESCRIBES HOW RAY AND JANE GARASSINO have landscaped their secluded hillside home. When they set about covering the bare earth, they discovered that whatever topsoil had once been there was gone, and bedrock was just two feet below the surface. Today, after considerable soil amendment, the home has a charming entry garden and an attractive mix of plant material on the hillside overlooking the couple's swimming pool. Unusual plants, such as the *Gunnera manicata* (an enormous-leafed bog plant from Brazil), thrive in a moist nook near the pool, shaded by the large deck.

"I understand the basic concepts of gardening," Ray explains, "but Freeland Tanner has taught me a lot. He helped with layouts and plant combinations. I think my favorite trees right now are the maples. He likes them, too. We have fun looking for plants at nurseries in Santa Rosa and Sonoma."

Describing the garden as eclectic, Ray waves his hand at the bright and interesting combination of plant specimens on the hillside. "I like natives, and this year I guess we've got about fifty oaks growing from acorns. Plus, we have flax, junipers, irises, roses, artemisia, *Helichrysum*, and *Euryops pectinatus*. I've put it all on drip irrigation." After work and on weekends, Ray, a vice president at Mondavi Winery, spends time in the garden, constantly tending and extending.

Ray motions toward a break in the trees near the front garden and says, "C'mere, I want to show you something." We walk into the cool, filtered light to see the beginnings of a shade garden.

"My dad was quite a gardener," Ray says, "and when he passed away about a year ago I dug up some of his favorite plants and moved them here, as a memorial to him." Besides the rhododendron, camellia, and azalea bushes Ray transplanted from his father's home in Menlo Park, there's a dogwood tree that the Mondavis contributed to the memorial garden.

Looks as if Ray's father has passed on more than plants; he passed his gardening genes to Ray, too. ❧

Springtime brings a flush of

blossoms to Fred Lyon's orchard of

crabapples, whose fallen petals

create a perfumed bed of pale pink.

This remarkable small garden feels

like an enclosed room roofed and

carpeted with blossoms. The size is

deceptive, its scale and proportion

so "right" it appears vast. The

layout reveals the critical eye of the

designer—a photographer—Fred

Lyon. LEFT: *A fiscus-covered arch*

frames the lavender-lined pathway

toward the outlying vineyards.

"MY GARDEN HAS CLASSIC BONES WITH INFORMAL PLANTS." SO SAYS FRED LYON OF HIS big little garden. The bones were showing and they were exceptional when I first visited in January. I was struck with how simple everything looked and yet how elegant. The garden exemplifies the well-known maxim that if you have a garden in January, you have a garden.

Not a large garden, but one with lots of interest, much of which comes from the form. The house itself has a sense of formality—it is basically a tall square with few windows; a creeping ficus almost completely covers it in year-round green. A geometric sculptural effect is created by the green vines, where they outline the tall, rectangular windows. On the street side, the vines stop just under the small two-foot-square windows sixteen feet off the ground. The house is extended by a high wall connecting it to the edge of the garden. Because the wall is entirely covered by the same ficus that grows on the house, it not only extends the house, but it extends the garden vertically. One of my favorite parts of the landscape is the ficus archway in this wall, which allows visitors to glimpse the garden. Right away, we see neat rows of different kinds of lavender and upright rosemary backed with roses. Then we see a hedge continuing the garden. We feel drawn to enter and discover more.

Even in winter this is a handsome and quiet place. Six pollarded fruitless mulberry trees on a concrete brick terrace allow the sun to enter the house during the dark winter months and provide welcome shade for the valley's all too hot summers. The rectangular swimming pool lines up on an axis with the house, beyond which stretches a large expanse of very green lawn in two levels. Bordering the lawn on three sides are rows of flowering fruit trees—a single row of Japanese crabapple trees on each side and a triple row of the same trees at the end. The view is extended under the branches of the fruit trees to the vineyard and the Mayacamas mountain range beyond.

OPPOSITE: *Whether in full blossom or, as seen above, thrusting bare branches to the sky in winter, the crabapples*

stand as monitors of the passing seasons. At one end of the garden, Fred uses his vineyard and the adjacent vineyards and

hills beyond to extend his rectangular room.

Lichens thrive on the trunks of pollarded fruitless mulberry trees on a concrete brick terrace fronting Lyon's architecturally strong home. Their silhouette is caught by the reflection in the long narrow windows. Fred has skillfully controlled our view with the landscaping. With your back to the house, and the help of hedges flanking both sides of the lawn, your eye is directed over the pool and out to the vineyards. The view is nearly unobstructed, filtered only by the fruitless crabapples, and a rose-entwined swag chain beyond. RIGHT: *Fred tends to garden maintenance.*

The entire garden is contained within a rectangle, but the visitor's eye travels with pleasure to the wisteria, the star jasmine, and the *Rosa banksiae*-covered trellis. Fred says a garden should never be boring. "Imperfection is the most important ingredient of perfection. Any great masterpiece has its imperfection. That's what keeps it immediate and authentic."

The moment of absolute heaven comes later in the year, when the flowering crabapples bloom. A day or two after full flower is majestic with delicate pale pink petals drifting silently down. I felt compelled to walk under the trees and become a part of the flowering. The perfume was heady and utterly intoxicating. Then a breeze came. I was covered with the lightest showering of petals, and I had the sensation of walking on newly fallen snow.

Fred and his late wife Ann created this home and garden with simple materials and with great style. They did most of the work themselves, and Fred says, as if it were a simple matter, "Oh yes, I can build treillage." He also does all his own vineyard work and was one of the first pioneers to use a drip system in the Napa Valley. He then applied the same labor- and water-saving device to his garden. Fred's studio is in San Francisco, and he's often away on photographic assignments all over the world. His garden is necessarily very efficient. "We had to design a garden that didn't need to be manicured, would exist on an automatic drip system, and would provide pleasure all year long."

LEFT: *A "see-through" gate*

expresses friendliness at the home of

Harold and Carol Green, where the

poolhouse wall becomes a fair-

weather art show. OPPOSITE: *The*

giant Spanish amphoras, originally

for storing wine, are used here in a

daring manner, adding a unique

theme to the garden. The top urn,

transformed into a fountain, diverts

the gaze of passersby on the main

street, while acting as a noise

buffer. Behind the rock baffle is a

path leading to the front door,

bounded on one side by short rows

of grapes, each of which ends in a

pink rose. LOWER RIGHT: *Potted*

asparagus ferns enrich a French-

style fountain area, whose bubbly

melody masks noise from the street.

WHEN CAROL AND HAROLD GREEN MOVED INTO THEIR home in 1989, the handsome old stone building that had housed the Esmeralda Winery over a century ago had undeniable charm—and equally undeniable landscape problems.

The home had been a weekend getaway for a succession of owners, and the front was decorated in a style that Carol refers to as "condo landscaping." The U-shaped driveway came straight from the street to the front door. There were some nondescript shrubs, and plenty of *Vinca minor,* which the Greens are still struggling to eradicate. Right away, they moved both the driveway and the garage to the side of the house, allowing a much more gracious entrance. "And it also freed up more space for the garden!" Carol adds.

"Although I'd gardened at our former home, where we had seven acres," she continues as we start a walking tour from the front gate, "I'd never done an entire landscape. But I couldn't find a professional who had the right feeling for this small garden.

"My goal with the outdoor structure was to set up individual garden rooms, so you couldn't see the whole thing at once. I wanted each space to have its own feel, so it would become a serendipitous experience. It's a strolling garden," she continues. "Here are the amphora urns, which are used for storing wine in Spain; then you see the found objects on the back wall of the garage; I've incorporated the rows of Cabernet grapevines into the garden, and the 'Just Joey' roses are on the opposite side; then there's the French fountain garden, and so on."

What she has created is the feeling of uncluttered tranquillity one might expect from a small estate in Provence. Topiary evergreens guard the entrance to the fountain garden where four young sycamore trees will eventually be pollarded to join limbs overhead. Close by is a restful conversation area where the relaxing sound of splashing water erases any street noise.

The unusual circular swimming pool, with a raised spa as its hub, heightens the holiday feeling of the setting. "You reach the spa on the footbridge, walking over water," Carol laughs. "You don't get to do that very often!" Shielding the pool from the neighbors are large plantings of bamboo, with Lady Banks' roses and wisteria for seasonal color.

A few years ago, the Greens' home was nominated for the local Landscape of the Year award, and it won. After the announcement, one of the judges called. "He told me he'd seen a lot of landscapes in his twenty-five years in the business," Carol smiles at the memory, "but nothing quite like ours. I considered that quite a compliment." ❦

THE NEW COLLECTORS

WHEN SOMEONE STARTS GARDENING AND IS THOROUGHLY BITTEN BY

THE GARDEN BUG, IT SEEMS THAT ONE MORE PLANT IS NEVER ENOUGH.

TWO OF THE GARDENERS IN THIS CHAPTER FIT INTO THAT CATEGORY—

LEXIE ELLSWORTH AND JOHN TRAULSEN—BUT THE TANNERS' AND

ROGER WARNER'S PASSION FOR ONE MORE PLANT COMES MORE

FROM A PROFESSIONAL INTEREST AND A BOTANICAL CURIOSITY

ABOUT UNUSUAL VARIETIES IN NEW COMBINATIONS OF PLANTING.

PREVIOUS PAGES: *The Ellsworths' tennis court lawn area.* ABOVE: *Freeland and Sabrina's garden is a botanical bombardment of rich texture and color. Framing the pool garden is a Japanese maple* (Acer palmatum *'Dissectum seriyu') and the white rose 'Happenstance,' with hostas above the rock, and Japanese Forest Grass* (Hakonechloa macra *'Aureola') against golden creeping Jenny. In the pond, pickerel rush thrives among hardy water lilies.* OPPOSITE: *The summer house with tall grass* (Miscanthus sinensis *'Variegatus'), yellow Italian cypress ('Swane's Golden'), and crape myrtle ('Petite Pinkie')—held together by bursts of* Verbena bonariensi.

THE PRINTED COCKTAIL NAPKINS THAT FREELAND AND Sabrina Tanner use when entertaining accurately sum up the feeling they have about their immaculate English cottage garden: "Gardening is not just another day at the plant." For the Tanners, who are both involved in landscaping professionally, it's a love affair.

Coming down the narrow drive, your first impression of the garden is that behind the lush foliage and the shingled roof of the gazebo there *must* be a thatched-roof cottage. "Yep, I wanted one," Freeland chuckles, "but the building codes here wouldn't allow it." Instead, they built this New England–style cottage.

Right away, you sense the house is of minimal importance. What's important here is the *landscape.* After clearing the land for construction of their home in 1987, the garden was laid out primarily to display the couple's collection of more than 150 heirloom rose bushes. It was then given the name Malmaison West, a tribute to Empress Josephine's famed rose garden in France.

But roses alone couldn't fulfill the Tanners' idea of what a garden should be. Japanese maples and dwarf conifers joined the mix, and suddenly there were ornamental grasses, perennials, bulbs, evergreen trees, shrubs, and modern roses—particularly the new David Austins. And beyond an arched wooden gate, the Tanners also maintain a raised-bed vegetable garden, designed for beauty as well as function.

As Freeland explains, the emphasis is on year-round color and texture in a small garden that includes a fish pond, two rock gardens, a gazebo, and several seating areas. The Tanners borrowed design ideas from both the traditional English cottage garden and the elegant eighteenth-century French parterres, and combining them into an asymmetrical format has created a look that Freeland calls "controlled chaos." The end result is both stimulating and engaging.

Entirely organic, Malmaison West is watered and fed through an automatic irrigation system, while landscape fabric and mulch in planting beds have kept weed problems to a minimum. Special efforts made to improve the clay soil before planting have paid off in good drainage patterns and healthy plants.

Most visitors suspect the Tanners have a full-time gardener, but they do all the work themselves. Freeland even designed and built the wooden structures within the garden. "We come out here together on weekends," says Sabrina, "and spend most of a day keeping things in order. It's really not much of a job, particularly when you enjoy being here."

It's true: gardening *is* more than just another day at the plant.

TOP: *My favorite parts of the garden, and where I think Freeland really excels, are his green areas— where only multiple shades and textures of green are shown.* ABOVE RIGHT: *Rose 'Charman', Jerusalem Sage (yellow* Phlomis fruticosa), Erysimum *'Bowles' Mauve' backed by blue Atlas Cedar and bird houses.* RIGHT: *An unusual* combination of Phormium *'Yellow Wave' against deep reddish* barberry (Berberis thunbergii *'Rose Glow').* ABOVE: *The smoke* bush (Cotinus coggygria *'Royal Purple') against the light yellow* Nicotiana *'Langsdorfie' and* Phormium *'Apricot Queen' gives punch to the giant* Delphinium *'Bluebird'.*

The quaint summer house provides a viewing place within the massive planting. Early morning sun catches the seed heads of the giant feather grass (Stipa gigantea) and golden maple. Cardoon and delphinium stretch for more sun while the lovely lilac iris and 'Bowles' Mauve' wallflower are content to show off their color. A willow arch invites us to explore more of the garden past the tricolor beech (Fagus sylvatica 'Tricolor'), while a blue spruce (Picea pungens 'Moerheimii') provides contrast to the rest of the greens.

OPPOSITE: *High on a hilltop, the Ellsworths have made the most of their view, with broad sweeps of lawn edged only by a very low wall. Beneath the olives, an exuberant mix of sun-loving plants thrives: white coneflowers, festuca, a deep pink cluster rose, and nepeta.* ABOVE: *This footpath to the front door affords Lexie the opportunity to experiment with a variety of draught-tolerant plants. Simple Mediterranean plantings of olives and rosemary seem right for the sunny pool garden.*

ALEXANDRA "LEXIE" ELLSWORTH IS A DEDICATED GARDENER WHO KNOWS WHAT SHE wants and how to get it. "I'm not gardening for other people," she says, "so if the end result doesn't work, it's only my problem."

When Bob and Lexie Ellsworth purchased their hillside Los Olivos (named for its wealth of olive trees), they hired landscape architect Jack Chandler to design the hardscape of the garden. Both are still singing his praises.

Chandler's use of buff-colored stucco throughout the landscape is striking. It delineates the cultivated garden by edging the expansive lawn with the wide sweep of a one-foot-high wall. It trims the terraced edges of another lawn area (reminding Lexie of rice paddies in the Philippines where she spent her childhood). And it makes an elegant procession between the garden and a wild boulder terrain in a set of long, broad steps.

Where Lexie stepped out on her own, though, was in plant selection, venturing to bring her vision to life more precisely. Thus began her education as a gardener. "Even before I fell in love with gardening, I knew what I wanted," she says. Roses intertwined with ivy spill over rock walls, yielding to nature's combination of scrub oaks and native plants beyond. Throughout the garden, from the intensive planting at the entrance to the path leading to the pool and all around the house, there is a wealth of unusual plant material. Pink flowering strawberries, cranesbills such as the hardy *Geranium endressii* 'Wargrave Pink', artemisias, and purple sage are just a few of the Ellsworths' favorites. (Yes, Bob has the garden bug, too.) Plantings of wavy *Gaura lindheimeri,* a three-foot perennial with white blossoms opening from pink buds, unify part of the landscape and give a sense of movement.

Lexie admits, "When I see a plant I don't have, I want to try it."

One gardening lesson Lexie learned quickly is that mixing native and non-native plants presents problems, because with rich soil and ample water, the natives rapidly outgrow everything else. "I'm just learning the balance," she says with a smile.

The tennis court area, hidden away on most properties, has become a marvelous landscape feature here because of a huge, handsome trellis of wood with concrete columns, a dramatic idea in its own right that also helps to obscure the view of the court. Nearby are more formal planted areas of shrub roses and climbers winding their way into the trees.

"Whenever I do a new area now, I get a professional with a sense of scale to lay it out," Lexie observes, "then I work with a local horticulturist to place the plants. It's less expensive, and I'm more satisfied."

Aside from her other passion, raising Morgan horses, Lexie buries herself in horticulture. "I love going to nurseries," she confesses, "and when a big one went out of business here recently, I came home with a cattle truck full of plants. I'll bet I spend at least five hours a day out in the garden, and I love every minute of it!" 🌱

Boulders add structure to the California hillside planting, while a bench provides a spot to enjoy the panoramic view of the Napa Valley below. The soft Stachys byzantina *'Big Ears' forms a striking contrast to the hard rock and spiky fescue and the creeping ivy ground cover (*Glechoma hederacea*).*

Oversized Mexican plates make

a dramatic table for entertaining in

a climate that permits outdoor

dining during much of the year.

Jack Chandler's skill is evidenced in

the design of the garden lights,

the broad sweeping entrance to the

house, and the brilliant disguise

of the tennis court with its stucco-

columned pergola. A long, low

wall emphasizes the edge of the tennis

court and creates a neatly con-

tained planting space.

TOP TO BOTTOM: Magnolia x soulangeana *'Rustica rubra'* *against the soaring roof of the gar-* *den house. The blooms of the China* *rose 'Le Vésuve' grace the garden* *from May to December. Inviting us* *to pause and enjoy the backlit tall* *apricot foxgloves* (Digitalis pur-*purea) *is the stylish Lutyens* *bench. In the foreground, the dark* *purple form of* Salvia haema-*todes *gives emphasis to the creamy* *white rose 'Windrush'.*

"UP THERE IS THE OLD OATHILL MINE ROAD, ACTUALLY THE most beautiful walk in Napa County, with over fifty different species of wildflowers along the trail," John Traulsen states as he points to the hillside that rises sharply beyond his property. In the 1986 Valentine's Day flood, a mudslide came down this hill requiring much of the vineyard and garden to be redesigned.

Touring the one and one-half acre garden with John, you get the impression that he and his wife, Patricia, felt an *obligation* to create beauty around their home to complement the natural state of the setting. And you quickly realize you are in the company of quite a plant connoisseur: "Here is a variegated kumquat," he points out, "and over there we've got a clump of yellow *Clivia.* That's a Himalayan birch, the whitest of the species. Our hedges are a bit unusual, too. At the back of the house is a hedge of miniature olives, one of a thornless *Elaeagnus,* and a new plant-ing of *Juniperus chinensis* 'Spartan', which will tolerate cold down to minus 10 degrees."

Landscape designer Roger Warner created the framework of the garden initially, and gave it a needed focal point by placing eleven nine-foot-tall cast pillars, looking like stone columns in a Roman forum, around the perimeter of the lawn in the planting area.

Multilayered beds confined in thick rock walls clearly reveal that John's favorite plants are roses. Over three hundred of them tumble, sprawl, and climb in a display of floral fireworks. He introduces guests to his roses as if he were a host at a cocktail party: "This is 'Fair Bianca', 'St. Cecilia', 'Cardinal de Richelieu', 'The Squire', 'The Prince', Lady Banks', and *Rosa primula,* noted for its scented foliage rather than its flowers."

During his forty-year career as a pharmacist, John says getting out in the garden "helped clear the cob-webs." Nowadays, dividing his time between his pas-sions of winemaking and gardening, you seldom hear him talk of cobwebs: "My problem," he laughs, "is that I keep getting more and more ideas." ❦

A David Austin rose, 'Cressida',
climbs the architectural stone-like
pillars arising from the lushly
planted curving border accented by
purple Salvia haematodes.
A voluptuous mix of roses flanks
stone steps (excavated from Far
Niente), which lead to a Mary
Tilden statue backed by moss roses.
Another David Austin, 'Mary Rose'
is in the foreground to the right.

OPPOSITE: *Setting the theme of the garden is the drama of clipped lavender mounds* (Lavandula intermedia 'Fred Boutin'), *harmonizing with lichen-clad*

oaks and Plecostachys serpyllifolia *in the foreground.* ABOVE: *The setting sun slides across the vineyards into the Kramlichs' garden and terrace. A Normandy*

Caen stone arch marks the entrance, punctuating the pathway lined in purple sage, bronze basil, Greek basil, and lavender.

WHEN I FIRST VISITED DICK AND PAM KRAMLICH SEVERAL YEARS AGO, MY LASTING impression was of driving in a long entrance past a gentle knoll of different kinds of oak trees to see masses of lavenders in several shades of purple enhanced by a finely textured, low-growing gray ground cover; tall, light gray *Teucrium;* and dark green rosemary.

I remember thinking how remarkable a limited color scheme could be when done in broad swaths. The garden was very beautiful and impressive then, but is even more dramatic today.

Current landscape designer Roger Warner followed Sarah Hammond, who introduced the original plant schemes, and Jack Chandler, who was responsible for giving function, character, and charm to the nondescript house with his trellises, terraces, new driveway, and designated parking areas.

When Roger, who sees with a broad vision, took over the garden design, he wisely left most of the basic planting but extended it in all directions and gave it a new interpretation. The lavenders, now tightly clipped, march in neat rows all the way to the front gate. He changed the character of the *Teucrium,* both the tall gray one (*Teucrium fruticans*), and the small dark green (*Teucrium chamaedrys*), by carefully sculpting them into near-perfect spheres.

When asked to describe the style that emerged, he answers, "It's a Pam Kramlich garden."

Today, a precision-made wall of cut fieldstone rimming the property lets us know that someone here is taking charge of nature. In front of the driftwood-colored main gates, free-form plantings of California poppies, brilliant chartreuse heads of *Euphorbia characias wulfenii,* and giant white-flowered Matilija poppies contrast sharply with the neatly sculpted rounds of lavender just inside. The compelling spheres in all sizes and shades of gray command your attention to the exclusion of all else. Finally, having played leap frog with your eye over each ball, you realize that an important element of the garden is

the softening light produced by the overhead oaks. What a different garden it would be without them. As you walk on, the cream-colored post-and-lintel arch beckons you farther.

Eyes and ears are drawn to the left, to water running over large boulders in the middle of a small lawn, pulling you toward it and then up a few steps to another small, irregularly shaped grass area. The quiet, soft green of the lawn captures the flickering light and shade beneath the trees and works as a lovely foil against the beautiful gray green textures of *Perovskia atriplicifolia,* and the clary sage (*Salvia sclarea* 'Turkestanica') contrasts with the darker green of foxglove (*Digitalis purpurea* 'Alba').

One of my favorite parts of the garden is Pam's natural, crescent-shaped design of boulders emerging gently from the lawn. Pam explains that the rocks just kept appearing from their surrounding vineyard. "We had to find places for them! We built a very long wall and then even used many of them imbedded in the earth to form a patio we now use as a dining area. Planting baby tears between the stones made them easier to walk on and created a cool-looking terrace."

Near the entertainment area, the edible garden begins. Herbs of all kinds abound, but with such discernment for textures and colors that they act as magnificent landscape plants, as well. Bronze basil

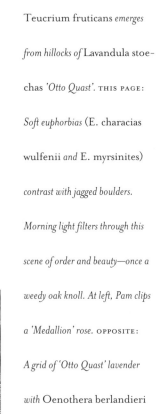

mixes with soft gray *Salvia officinalis* 'Berggarten'; chartreuse marjoram stands beside dark green thyme. Vegetables are plentiful and beautiful: red and green chard, purple and white eggplants, bright tomatoes. Last year, Pam and Dick finished their outdoor kitchen, complete with a gas-burning stove and a stone pizza oven, where their friend Paul Bertolli comes and cooks with delicacies from the vegetable garden he helped design.

Walking along the edge of the garden, a handsome planting of blue purple catmint beneath apple trees leads past a glorious hillside where some three thousand 'Victoria Falls' irises hold their heads high.

The west side of the house, hot and sunny, is the natural location for the pool and roses. Except for the floppy, natural-looking 'Icebergs', the roses are hidden, so as not to interrupt the serenity of the large lawn edged in rosemary and the rural, peaceful view. On the bank below are hundreds of Pam's favorite picking roses, planted, of course, in neatly curved rows.

To the casual observer, the garden scheme appears simple because the color palette gives greens a major emphasis and plants appear in generous groupings. But on closer inspection one finds a myriad of unusual plant varieties combined with great sensitivity and taste. The garden looks and feels loved by all its caretakers. Roger gives a lot of credit to Luis Peña and Javier Galvan who, with pride and precision, hand-clip all those hundreds of spheres, four times a year.

"This garden has a lot to do with interpreting Pam's wishes," Roger concludes. "I'm more an instrument than a creator." But Pam disagrees. "He's a genius," she says. No matter who took the lead, they're creating a most memorable garden. ❧

PREVIOUS PAGES: *The huge Teucrium fruticans emerges from hillocks of* Lavandula stoechas *'Otto Quast'.* THIS PAGE: *Soft euphorbias* (E. characias wulfenii *and* E. myrsinites) *contrast with jagged boulders. Morning light filters through this scene of order and beauty—once a weedy oak knoll. At left, Pam clips a 'Medallion' rose.* OPPOSITE: *A grid of 'Otto Quast' lavender with* Oenothera berlandieri *'Woodside White'.*

OPPOSITE: *Mounds of lavender seem to wander under the oaks.*

RIGHT: *Two man-made forms, the rounded* Teucrium *and the linear vineyard rows, dramatize their geometries against each other. A boulder of* Teucrium *is the result of meticulous pruning. The overall effect of this well-designed garden is rhythmic harmony with a fascinating plant collection.*

NEXT MILLENNIUM SPACES

A FEW OF OUR NAPA VALLEY GARDENS WERE CREATED TO COMPLEMENT

INNOVATIVE HOUSE DESIGNS—DESIGNS THAT COMBINE ENVIRONMEN-

TAL SENSITIVITY WITH ABSTRACT OR STYLIZED SCULPTURAL FEATURES.

WHETHER IT BE THE HIGH-TECH OF STARK, ANGLED WALLS THAT

CHANGE COLOR WITH THE SEASONS, THE LOW-TECH OF A BUILDING

STYLE WITH TEN-THOUSAND-YEAR-OLD ROOTS, OR THE TRANSFORMA-

TION OF EXTERIOR SPACES INTO SHOWCASES FOR MODERN ART, THESE

GARDENS INSPIRE NEW IDEAS FOR THE TWENTY-FIRST CENTURY.

ART, ARCHITECTURE, SCULPTURE, AND HORTICULTURE have been skillfully combined in Marion Greene's garden to combat an adversary few visitors think of as a problem in the Napa Valley: heat.

One-half of Marion's garden is within stone walls that reflect the sunshine and intensify the stress on the plants. Originally this area was used for parking in front of her home, an old stone winery that has been converted into an avant-garde dwelling combining Napa Valley history with the cutting edge of interior design. "It looked like a used car lot. I hated it, but I had accepted it," Marion explains. "But then my son (Byron Kuth, a San Francisco architect) said, 'You're crazy! We can't let them park here!'"

Following his advice, several olive trees were brought in to soften the angular lines of the area. He also created a handsome, industrial-looking steel pergola that is most dramatic under night lighting. During the daytime it provides shade, being a framework for climbing vines.

In front of the building, one area of the garden the heat cannot harm is startlingly simple and dramatic. Perimeter hedges create a room for a single heirloom oak on a raked gravel floor. Besides three cypresses in the corner, the only addition is a marvelous six-foot-tall acorn sculpture in slate, created on site by Scottish sculptor Andy Goldsworthy, in tribute to the carpet of acorns that covered the ground during his visit.

Landscapers Roger Warner and Ron Lutsko have both had an influence on the development of the garden, but Marion says she's gained enough confidence from these professionals to make her own decisions about the landscape. "I think Roger is one of the most talented designers in the Valley," she affirms, "and Ron has been helpful in bringing unusual plant material, such as euphorbias, into the blue and white garden."

When a silver lace vine fried in the summer heat, Marion replaced it with hop vines, which will tolerate high temperatures. 'White Texas' redbuds are used to best effect against a blue wall. Other plants that shrug off the ravages of summer temperatures include ceanothus, mock orange, yellow daylilies, mulberry trees, an old *Rosa banksiae* planted twenty years ago, and a wide variety of fruit trees that have been espaliered on architectural steel frames on an adjoining piece of property. This mix of high-tech art and landscape make this property unique and expresses Marion's adventuresome spirit and broad taste.

And now she is gathering a collection of horticultural books to house in the lower room of the circular tower. She plans to have it open for interested gardeners to come and enjoy reading so that they can share her passion. ❧

PREVIOUS PAGES: *Jack Chandler's entrance.* ABOVE: *A wide decomposed granite border under the olives echoes the form of Greene's rectangular pool. The circular tower is the future home of a horticultural library. A narrow canal at the base of the blue wall is used both architecturally and horticulturally. Guarding the pool is a stone jaguar from Mexico.*

OPPOSITE: *Andy Goldsworthy's acorn sculpture shares a courtyard with its papa, a lofty oak.*

OPPOSITE: *The garden chess-*

board. THIS PAGE: *Blooming*

lavender and Teucrium

chamaedrys *divide the terrace*

from the pool area. Fountain

grass (Pennisetum setaceum)

catches the dawn light. The

stone columns reflected in the pool

create a unity with the terrace

above. Jack Chandler's sculpted

metal chess pieces are poised for the

next move.

RIDING IN AN AUTOMOBILE WITH LANDSCAPE ARCHITECT AND SCULPTOR JACK CHANDLER to inspect his clients' gardens tells you a lot about the man and how he works: he knows exactly where he's going, the fastest way to get there, and how to have fun along the way.

As evening approaches the villa at Longmeadow Ranch and we get out of the car, Chandler observes, "This was once asphalt, right up to the front door. And the house was stark and bare. I like a sense of entry in my gardens. So we transplanted some full-grown olive trees that were nearby to create a bridge of branches to soften that space a little."

Longmeadow Ranch was built in the 1920s using basalt rock found on the property. Chandler expanded upon the home's strong Italian feel by erecting stone columns of the same rock. He also added a unique entertainment area that transforms a small manicured lawn into an oversized chess board with dramatic, two-foot-high black metal chess pieces, which he designed and created. "It's fun being a garden-maker *and* sculptor," Chandler enthuses. What led him to this innovation? "The owners like to play chess," he says, "so I sculpted this chess set, and we have room on the stone steps of the new arbor for people to watch the game in action."

As in traditional Italian gardens, floral color is kept to a minimum in the landscape with white 'Iceberg' roses that seem to be continually in bloom. "I think of this as a nice, peaceful garden with an Old World flavor to it," Chandler says. "And once the grapes work their way up and over the arbor, it really will be handsome." 🌿

171

ABOVE: *Both the landscaping and the architecture at Jack Chandler's home exhibit a sense of restraint, with the emphasis on structural elements. With minimal planting around the house, the tree-covered hills and vineyards fill in the landscape.* OPPOSITE: *Autumnal grasses and bare poplars accentuate the stark simplicity of this contemporary house. The changing hour of the day paints white stucco walls with luminous color.*

EXPLAINING HIS APPROACH TO LANDSCAPING, JACK CHANDLER SAYS, "I DESIGN A LOT WITH straight lines, and some clients feel that concept is too angular. But a garden needs structure, and when you get the plants to soften it, the angular feeling disappears. And once a garden has good structure it will endure almost anything."

A clear example of what Jack is talking about is his own garden, where uninterrupted stretches of vibrant green lawn are edged with young trees that frame the two-story white stucco home's ultramodern style of architecture. "I wanted a stylized, sculptural garden using plant materials as masses," he says. "It's all on a grid, so the horizontal walls work well, and the pond is a balancing element."

Then there's the three-foot wall that goes all the way around the property: "That's my snake wall," he grins. "The first year we were here, we killed thirty-two rattlers. The next year there were twenty-eight, then fewer and fewer. If they get in over this wall," he laughs, "I'm going to turn the title over to them!"

Ironically, Chandler found his own garden one of his greatest challenges. The soil is very poor, no more than a few inches deep over rock. The water contains boron, which spells death to acid-loving plants. The creeping red fescue lawn bordering his large workshop studio creates toxins that affect growth rates on the newly planted trees.

"What I'm yearning for," he sighs, "is an English country garden. In my next house, if I don't have the soil for that, I'm going to bring in two feet of good dirt and make it work!" ❧

DEVA GARDENS

MACHAELLE SMALL WRIGHT PUT FORTH THIS EXPANSIVE DEFINITION OF

A GARDEN: "WHERE THERE IS FORM, THERE IS NATURE. WHERE NATURE

AND HUMANS INTERACT, THERE IS A GARDEN. WHERE THERE IS A GAR-

DEN, THERE IS AN IMPLIED CO-CREATIVE PARTNERSHIP." MORE AND

MORE PEOPLE ARE BEGINNING TO UNDERSTAND NATURE NOT AS A THING

TO BE CONQUERED, BUT AS AN ENERGY TO BE OBSERVED AND LISTENED

TO. THE WORD *DEVA* DESCRIBES A LEVEL OF CONSCIOUS INTELLIGENCE

WITHIN NATURE. DEVAS ARE THE PLANT KINGDOM'S EQUIVALENT OF

ANGELS—GUIDES AND MESSENGERS. IF YOU BELIEVE THAT PLANTS HAVE A

LIFE FORCE OR A SPIRIT, A DEVA, THEN ALL GARDENS ARE DEVA GAR-

DENS. IN THIS SECTION, WE HAVE INCLUDED ONLY A FEW OF THE MANY

GARDENERS WHO SEEM TO ACKNOWLEDGE THE SECRET LIFE OF PLANTS.

PREVIOUS PAGES: A winter day at Chappellet. ABOVE: Hiding only the "knees of the grapevines" but not the view, a

four-foot wall makes a smooth curve around the entrance courtyard, separating the vineyard from the home. OPPOSITE:

The encircling wall is anything but isolating. With its low height and multiple entryways, it is welcoming.

AT THE END OF A LONG DRIVE THROUGH ROWS OF 'BLOODGOOD' SYCAMORES LIES AN inviting scene—what appears to be a traditional hacienda. A low-slung tile-roofed house with ancient weeping willows is enclosed in a circular wall. Upon closer inspection, the French doors with brown wooden shutters and the flag-stone paving around the pool make the house seem perhaps more French or Italian than Spanish.

It is a surprise to learn that this well-established garden was created only a few years ago. This good-looking and functional compound was originally the result of a collaborative effort of Napa Valley landscaper Jack Chandler, New York interior designer Tom Britt, and San Francisco architect Karl G. Smith.

Chandler designed the circular wall to create an entrance to the house and planted more trees to fulfill the owners' desire for "shade and solace." As Chandler explains, "A four-foot-high wall permits a view of the surrounding vineyards but hides the knees of the grapevines."

The dramatic gateless opening, defined by tall wisteria-draped pillars capped with a large square wooden lintel, provides a welcoming entrance to what is really an enormously inviting outdoor room. Three other similarly styled but scaled-down openings keep the wall from feeling restrictive in any way, so that, in fact, the overall sense is one of safe haven and friendliness. Soft birches and sycamores extend that ambience to the far side of the house.

Tom Britt added style with the oversized lanterns he found to punctuate the entrances to the courtyard and the garden. Repeats of large, unusual sandstone pots next to the house were also his addition. Smith, the architect, was able to turn an undistinguished tract house into a charming European-looking country house with a red tile roof. Then along came Peter Coates, the well-known English landscaper, who suggested that cypress and magnolias be planted between the vineyard and the lawn to break up the view and "to give a sense of dignity." Today, Becke Oberschulte is in charge of the garden and adds her knowledge and

femininity in the flower borders, with plants like peonies, oakleaf hydrangeas, and a host of other perennials.

Around 1985, the owners decided that the property, which was in terrible shape, "needed taming," so work began—on the vineyard, the house, and the garden. The garden, however, soon proved to have a life of its own. According to the family, it seemed as though the garden was aware that they had not made a commitment to be permanent residents, and so made its own decisions, saying, "I'll do what I need to do for you." It became a kind of courtship, complete with struggles and challenges. As the owners accepted that they were not the ones in charge but simply tenants, like the robins and blue jays, the garden began to open up its secrets. Harmony crept into their lives and into the garden as well. And the garden has blessed the participants, from the family to the devoted Mexican workers who have tilled and prayed over the land.

Now when you enter that high arch of the courtyard with the sunlight streaming in through the weeping willow, it is alive with energy and serenity. ❦

OPPOSITE: *The center circle was designed around this magnificent weeping willow—the tallest I've ever seen. The courtyard becomes enchanted as the liquid light of a low sun filters through its branches. Adjacent to the house, the gracious terrace with its flagstone paving is a perfect place to entertain. Corinthian capitals used as pedestals for large overflowing pots, along with the oversized terra-cotta pots of clipped ficus, add style to the outdoor living room.* RIGHT: *Lavender-colored* Wisteria floribunda *'Cook's Purple' drapes over a back gate beneath a native big leaf maple. A single canna blossom and wisteria limb are studies in color and form.*

ABOVE: An example of the wild informality of this garden. Masses of tall salvia 'Purple Majesty' offset peach-colored dahlias, with a brilliant hotspot of orange. Bob and Carol both enjoy this jubilant garden. OPPOSITE: The coral family of roses are great mixers—they go with pinks or oranges. A single open rose can be a complete bouquet or can add depth to a mixed arrangement.

WHEN NOTED ENGLISH GARDEN WRITER MIRABEL OSLER paid a visit to my garden on Pritchard Hill, she observed, "When I see a garden, I can pretty much tell what kind of person has made that garden." With that in mind, most people visiting Carol Grant's Secret Garden visualize her as the aunt they all wish they had—one who encourages romping through the garden, touching and smelling everything, and feeding rose blossoms to the quarter horse (appropriately named Rosey).

And, happily, that's just the kind of person she is.

Carol's garden is full and lush—so much so that the absence of even dozens of the rose blossoms she cuts is not noticeable. This is convenient, since Carol has now made a small business of her plants and cut flowers. At pruning time, she simply takes cuttings of her favorites and pokes them in the soil where she wants them. "I used to do it by the books with the potting soil, the RooTone, and all that, but I haven't time for it now," Carol explains. And magically, everything she puts in the ground grows.

Together with roses by the score are whatever other flowers catch her fancy. Foxgloves, Johnny-jump-ups, pansies, violets, verbenas, irises . . . you name it, it's in there. Somewhere.

Part of her enthusiasm for growing plants, she says, stems from the days when she was an instructor at Napa College, teaching sociology and philosophy.

"I always wanted people of all colors to learn to live together in harmony. And I think my garden is the society I was never able to reach in real life. All colors grow together."

Any concept of neat rows has long been abandoned as the community of flowers creates its own pathways. And no one ever complains, because in finding a route through the garden, one invariably stumbles upon some hidden treasure or a particular view that makes any inconvenience more than worthwhile.

Thirty years ago, Carol and her husband Bob bought the old homestead where, as a child, she had gardened with her mother. "It had been leased after my mother's death," she explains, "and when we moved in, it was surrounded with shoulder-high weeds. I wanted to find my mother's garden."

Although the search for that secret garden uncovered some planting beds outlined with stones, she was only able to find two of her mother's beloved roses. "And unconsciously, I just kept planting roses." David Austin roses now sprawl all the way down the hillside toward the chicken coop and a formidable tangle of blackberry brambles. "Now I have more than a thousand rose bushes," Carol says with a wide smile, "and I'm still planting." ❦

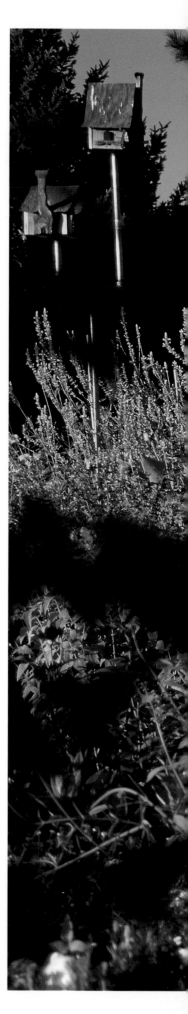

Spontaneous plantings of roses,

Salvia uliginosa, *daisies, dahlias,*

and other salvias mix and mingle,

spoiling the visitor with delights in

"Aunt Carol's" garden. No rows,

parterres, beds of one color, or

well-defined paths here. No bound-

aries. A sense of generosity and joy

in this free-formed garden abounds.

Plants are so vibrant they seem to

have a life of their own.

The front entrance already sets the mood of the garden with its dogwood tree, well-proportioned columns, and an inviting chair. OPPOSITE: *With the house*

situated on a knoll, the distant hills and valley become part of the landscape. The golden leaves of the tulip tree collected in patterns by the wind weave a path we

want to follow. A white kitty is spotlit by the sun as it basks near the kitchen door.

I REMEMBER WHEN MARY ANN MCGUIRE MCCOMBER PLANTED POPLARS AND PINE trees on the long driveway climbing up to her knoll. If I close my eyes, I can still see her driving down to water the new trees bucket by bucket. This kind of devotion is displayed in both the growth of the garden and of the woman herself. Now, twenty-seven years later, as the Reverend Mary Ann, she is more a student of the garden than ever before.

One of the most important features of the property is that it was sacred ground for Native Americans, perhaps even a burial site. "We have a great reverence for the American Indian legacy," explains Mary Ann, "and we have collected and turned over many artifacts to U.C. Berkeley. There's a special energy here, and we feel obligated to preserve it.

"Instead of bringing in a bulldozer and leveling the top of the hill, we worked with the natural contours." The house was designed to fit the existing site and, as a consequence, the handsome shingle-roofed adobe now hugs the ground and feels like an integral part of the landscape.

Mary Ann embraces a traditional Japanese tenet: when a visitor passes through the gate of the garden, a blessing sweeps away all cares. And here, when you enter under a tall arch with a cross and the inscription, "Family Home," you sense you are entering a spiritual place. "We want to create a sanctuary where people can relax and be healed," she says. "Many times people who come here are in crisis or have had some loss. They are wounded and hurting; it seems the garden opens us all to the harmony of nature. You know," she continues, "the first recorded garden was in a monastery, and the work of building it was a spiritual discipline."

The plantings on the drive up the hillside are all natives—ceanothus, rockrose, manzanitas, and oaks. The oaks continue into the driveway and all around the house, lending a sense of connectedness between the landscaped and the natural areas. On the far side of the house, a cooling green lawn shaded by large tulip trees (*Liriodendron tulipifera*) provides a quiet plateau above the farmlands and vine-

yards. At the edge of the lawn, under a loquat tree, a simple bench encourages meditation. And just a few feet away, down a path to the dark oval pool, is a marvelous area full of energy and beauty. Plants like *Verbena bonariensis, Scabiosa,* a pale yellow single rose, morning glory, and rosemary thrive in a joyous rhythm.

Reverend Mary Ann speaks of watching the cycles of energy come and go, and how certain spots seem to communicate more. "You have to ask—to acknowledge—to receive. When you work with the land with special intentions, it responds."

This place has been blessed by practitioners of many spiritual disciplines. His Holiness the Dalai Lama has been here with his blessing. Reverend Mary Ann adds, "We ask people when they come for a retreat to leave their blessing for those who come later." 🌼

A successful planting of tall
purple verbena (Verbena
bonariensis), *a yellow rose,*
California poppies, blue morning
glory, and rockrose vibrate on a
hillside between the swimming pool
and house. A different scene of
tranquillity is found at the edge of
the lawn under the sacred loquat
tree. Red-hot pokers (Kniphofia
uvaria) *sing out like a clarinet on*
a silent stage. Even the cat wears a
halo in this holy place.

Our garden sits on the edge of this

awe-inspiring vista of Lake

Hennessey and the Napa Valley. A

view is a free garden—you don't have

to own it to enjoy it. This vast scene

dwarfs conventional plants and

planting schemes. It takes drifts of

bearded iris, left, to make an impact.

Nature herself, however, makes the

biggest impact, constantly changing

our scene with dramatic light and

banks of fog. OPPOSITE: *Valerian*

(Centranthus ruber and

Centranthus r. 'Albus').

I AM HOPELESSLY IN LOVE WITH THE EARTH AND EVERY-thing it produces. The love affair, they tell me, began when I was two years old, making gingerbread mud pies. Apparently I slipped and fell in the mud, came up laughing, and proceeded to cover myself in the wet, gooey earth, rubbing it all over my arms and legs. Today, above all else I love working in the garden. It is an enormous magnet for me—a constant tug that says come out and play! My children even used to call the garden "mother's playpen."

When you arrive at our home on Pritchard Hill, you see vineyards steeply terraced on all sides of the house, the lake below, hills all around, the Napa Valley, and distant mountain ranges beyond. For me, the panorama is the garden, so in laying out our small piece of it I wanted it to flow into the vista, to belong. We used the rounded forms we saw in the hills and chose colors that would echo the gray greens of the oaks and lavender hues of the mountains.

Ours is not so much a "look-at garden" as a "work-in/walk-in garden." From its beginnings thirty years ago as a survival patch to feed our large family, farm help, and visitors, it has been essentially a working garden with an extensive vegetable plot and fruit orchard. Over the years, the garden has changed and grown with us, and presently includes an olive hill, herb garden, swimming pool, rose hill, and large dining terrace.

Directly off the terrace, on center stage, the vegetable garden is laid out in a large semicircle, divided into five sections. I believe that vegetables are as beautiful as any landscape plant, and that they should never be hidden away. For many years we planted in rows, all radiating out from the terrace, but now the garden is much more free-form. This year one area has circular mounds of squash, eggplant, corn, and root vegetables. Another section has rows of twelve different kinds of lettuce, alternating with bronze basil and lavenders. The third section is Jon-Mark's (middle son, thirty-something) tomato plot. He has a vegetable garden in Oakland, but he needed a little more space. The final two sections have been converted to cutting gardens.

To me, however, the most exciting part of the landscape is the wild garden. Situated below the semicircle and melding into the edge of the vineyard, is an area about four hundred feet long by forty feet wide. It grows itself without water other than rainfall. It all began when I was busy writing *A Vineyard Garden* and had not worked in the garden for

some time. Artichokes had cast their seeds here. My French *fenouil* spread itself around along with its friend, the bronze fennel. Feverfew daisies and several other flowers had reseeded themselves. When I saw how beautiful it was, I decided to encourage a few other volunteer candidates. Roger Warner brought some plants over and suggested we really make a garden here. He introduced the giant nicotine plant, *Nicotiana sylvestris, Salvia sclarea* 'Turkestanica', *Linaria, Campanula persicifolia*, and *Lavatera thuringiaca* 'Barnsley'.

The wild garden suits the needs of both my work and my spirit. First of all, it thrives on neglect. That's my kind of garden! Second, it is dramatic in scale and provides unusual material for arrangements. Third, it is constantly changing, with three distinct cycles, each more spectacular than the last. From the low, neat and tidy, monochromatically green stage to the grand finale, when the artichokes and cardoons suddenly burst into glorious purple thistles and everything in the garden looms above head height—the place begs for exploration. As I walk through the path coated with flat, black grape pomace, I enter under the artichokes' arch. I follow along to the edge where I suddenly encounter the entire vista of vineyard, valley, Lake Hennessey, and Mount St. Helena. Then, having an option which direction to look, I choose one where something far in the distance calls my attention—white massive plantings of giant Matilija poppies. I'm distracted by the inviting, dark, feathery path to my right. As I follow through the fennel forest, it gently caresses me with its velvet-like arms, and I come upon a dramatic cluster of pink and lavender clary sage mounted against a backdrop of the upper vineyard. There's no way out; I must retrace my steps and continue on another path. Here and there I see glimpses of light green and white nicotiana or more tall salvias at a distance. The artichokes have begun to flower, so occasional brilliant purple thistling heads shout for attention. As I continue, I begin to emerge out of Alice's secret garden to the rest of the world. Rock walks, old-fashioned roses, and tomato plants bring me slowly back to reality.

Each day, no matter what the demands of time, I try to spend a few moments walking in the magical wild garden to see what kinds of surprises await me. I'm never disappointed, and often find myself saying, "Oh, where did you come from?" or "Oh, how exquisite." Having read about Findhorn years ago, I can hear and feel the devas and pans everywhere. I know I'm not in charge. The garden is on its own and I am a bystander applauding the show. I certainly do not possess this garden, but it *does* possess me—and I *love* it. 🌱

In twenty-five years, five Matilija poppy plants have become a "bed," now one hundred feet by fifteen feet and still growing. Their only water is rainfall. BELOW LEFT: Used ornamentally as well as for food, light green lettuce and opal basil are planted between the rows of lavender. MIDDLE: Bronze leaf lettuce, light green 'Lollo biondo', and romaine begin to go to seed. RIGHT: If not picked for eating, artichokes burst to this glorious purple thistle.

LEFT: *Large euphorbia blossoms balance well with the two-foot plumes of the clary sage. It's easy to see that the vineyard is the most important part of my garden.*

BELOW LEFT: *The light green Feverfew daisy* (Chrysanthemum parthenium) *plays nicely against the* Verbena tenusecta *and lavender foliage.* OPPOSITE TOP, LEFT TO RIGHT: Verbascum olympicum, *with 'Love in a Mist'* (Nigella damascena), *and California poppies; valerian; a tree peony; and* Salvia sclarea Turkestanica. *(I know I've said "favorite" more than once, but peonies are my* real *favorite. The old-fashioned one here—planted sixty years ago—has been watered only by rainfall.)* BOTTOM: *Bearded iris ('Peach Spot') shows off well with deep pink valerian. Lavender and white iris ('Dancer's Veil') reinforce the tricolor lavatera.*

GRACE NOTES

IN MANY WAYS, THE ENTIRE NAPA VALLEY IS A GARDEN, WITH ITS

BACKDROP OF TREE-COVERED MOUNTAINS, ITS OLD AND NEW

STONE WALLS, AND ITS LUSH VINEYARDS. THE LANDSCAPING OF

OUR WINERIES IS AS INDIVIDUAL AS THE GARDENS WE HAVE JUST VIS-

ITED. SOME HAVE ELABORATE PLANTING. MANY HAVE EXTENSIVE

VEGETABLE GARDENS. OTHERS PRESENT GRACIOUS TREE-LINED

ENTRANCES. CHAPPELLET WELCOMES VISITORS WITH BOLD BOUL-

DERS. AND AT CLOS PEGASE, MODERN SCULPTURE TAKES THE

PLACE OF TREES. THESE WINERY GARDENS, UNLIKE THE PRIVATE

ONES, ARE AVAILABLE TO EVERYONE; ALONG WITH PASTORAL

VIEWS OF OLD WATER TOWERS, HISTORIC BARNS, GRAZING CATTLE,

AND OTHER TREASURES YOU MIGHT DISCOVER ON YOUR OWN

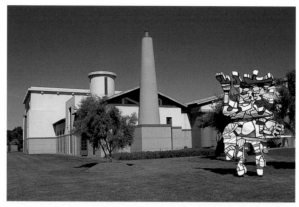

1st row: Niebaum-Coppola fountain entrance; Clos Pegase Winery and sculpture garden.

2nd row: Chimney Rock Winery; Robert Sinskey Vineyards.

3rd row: Martini Winery garden courtyard; Cakebread Cellars; Caymus Vineyards. 4th row: Beringer Winery vegetable and herb garden; barn on Spring Street.

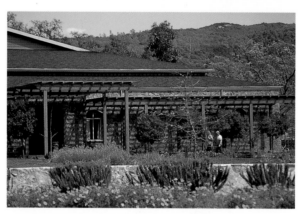

1ST ROW: *Hess Collection Winery garden; Raymond Winery entrance gate; Sterling Vineyards entrance.* 2ND ROW: *Robert Mondavi Winery arch; Peju Province Winery sculpture court.* 3RD ROW: *Franciscan Vineyards entrance; Beaulieu entrance; V. Sattui Winery.* 4TH ROW: *Sutter Home Winery entrance; Rutherford Hill Winery entrance.* FOLLOWING PAGE, TOP LEFT: *Al Brounstein developed this lake at his Diamond Creek Winery.* TOP RIGHT: *The stone walls of Stag's Leap Wine Cellars are a perfect backdrop for fields of wild flowers.* CENTER, LEFT: *Boulders greet guests at the entrance to Chappellet Winery.* BOTTOM: *Bright sunflowers adorn the vegetable gardens at the Robert Mondavi Winery. At Domaine Chandon, visitors enter over a bridge crossing these quiet ponds.*

❊ On a hilly terrain with little to work with, create terraces that act as large containers that you can fill with the proper soil; then you can do what you want.

DAGMAR SULLIVAN
❊ When you have a strong underlying structure you don't need a lot of color.

BLANCHE MONDAVI
❊ Plant the 'Simplicity' rose, which is a prolific bloomer. Don't prune; shear off dead blossoms instead.

MARY NOVAK
❊ Mulch roses after feeding them with alfalfa pellets. Add epsom salts (magnesium sulfate) to encourage more basal breaks and better branching.
❊ When you acquire a new property, live there for one year before ripping anything out.

ERIKA HILLS
❊ Every woman should have a 'Don Juan' rose and a 'Fantasy' grape in her life.

CHOTSIE BLANK
❊ Keep transition areas in the same palette as the main garden, to produce a flow between sections and unity overall.
❊ Don't believe anyone who says there's such a thing as a low-maintenance garden.

RON BIRTCHER
❊ Thanks to nature, a garden is in transition constantly. Learn your garden's strengths and shortcomings and adapt to them, then *fine-tune* on a small scale at every season.

LILA JAEGER
❊ Garden for enjoyment! Don't be a perfectionist.

GIL NICKEL AND JONATHAN PLANT
❊ When landscaper Jonathan Plant was first being interviewed, Gil Nickel asked him, "What does it take to create a world-class garden?" Plant answered, "Forty years." "Well, then," Gil responded, "we'd better get started."

KATIE TREFETHEN
❊ Leave cuttings on the grass and fertilize only twice a year.
❊ If kneeling and bending gets to be too hard on tired joints, put container plants, including bonsai trees, on a table and keep gardening!

ALICE GONSER
❊ If you plan to let your hedges grow high, plant something full at the base that will fill in as the hedge foliage goes upward. We planted hydrangeas, and the hedging still looks full and terrific.

ALEX PHILLIPS
❊ Look a lot at other gardens for ideas, study and think before planting, and if something works, plant *more* of it.

K. C. CUNNINGHAM
❊ Fill waist-high raised beds with vegetables and flowers so you can go on gardening until you're in your hundreds!

BECKY HUDSON
❊ Pay attention to texture; it gives a quality of excitement.

DEDE WILSEY
❊ When designing a garden, draw a map, paste pictures on it, and fill it in with crayons to see how the garden can come to life.

ANNIE FISHER
❊ Let your imagination go wild, then simplify your dream plan.

MARIA MANETTI FARROW
❊ Computerize your garden maintenance. Divide the garden into sections and, on a computer printout, describe each area, its irrigation needs, fertilization program, and day-to-day care.

STELLA WILSON
❊ Save fruit pits to plant new trees.
❊ Extend your annuals with water. In mild climates, petunias and impatiens can often go two or three seasons.

PETER NEWTON

❋ The adage that you should be ready to spend as much on the hole as on the tree is dead true. Be sure to really firm up the soil base under the center of the tree, so that the crown doesn't sink as it grows.

❋ Every plant brought home from a nursery needs care in siting and patience in planting. The plant never faces a more traumatic experience.

BILL HEWITT

❋ You must really *care* about the garden, and give *constant maintenance* to what you're doing. When you do that, the rewards are wonderful! And don't forget to irrigate!

JANIE CAFFERATA

❋ With patience, care, and hard work, you can coax a beautiful garden to evolve almost anywhere. Pass on the joy of gardening to your children—not just the chores. That's what my mother did for me.

MARGRIT MONDAVI

❋ As a welcoming note, put a fragrant planting at the front door.

DAPHNE ARAUJO

❋ For the good of the overall effect, throw out the extraneous, even if it happens to be a favorite.

RAY GARASSINO

❋ Oaks grow well from acorns! Plant today!

FRED LYON

❋ Experiment. If a plant does well, put in more. If it doesn't, rip it out and never look back.

CAROL GREEN

❋ Set up individual garden rooms, so you can't see the whole landscape at once.

FREELAND TANNER

❋ Landscape fabric and mulch in planting beds keep weed problems to a minimum; then water and feed through an automatic irrigation system.

LEXIE ELLSWORTH

❋ Don't mix native and nonnative plants in rich, well-watered soil.

❋ Get a professional to help you develop a sense of scale; work with a local horticulturist to place plants.

JOHN TRAULSEN

❋ Establish a focal point in every garden.

PAM KRAMLICH

❋ Baby tears between terrace stones make them easier to walk on.

JACK CHANDLER

❋ Create a good structure; then a garden will endure almost anything.

❋ Have fun along the way!

CAROL GRANT

❋ Want roses? Take cuttings of your favorites. Poke them in the soil wherever you want them, water them, and expect miracles.

MARY ANN McGUIRE McCOMBER

❋ Take the time to stop and enjoy what you and nature have created. Be still in your garden so you can experience its dynamics—what goes on there—the animals, the changing plants, the perfumes, the birds, the seasons. A garden is a sanctuary. If you are in need of healing, go to the garden.

MAI ARBEGAST, LANDSCAPE DESIGNER

❋ Think big and plant trees! They give a better, more lasting effect quicker than you might think. Plant thickly; thin quickly! If more people planted trees, we'd have a much nicer overall landscape.

ROGER WARNER, LANDSCAPE DESIGNER

❋ Most importantly, consider the climate and your available water supply—then design from there for comfort. And marry someone with a lot of money!

ACKNOWLEDGMENTS

Most authors agree, it takes a village to write a book. Our heartfelt thanks first of all both to the people who work the soil and the dreamers who create the work, and to the gardeners whose landscapes don't appear in the book, who opened their private gardens for numerous visits during the changing seasons.

Daniel D'Agostini, Nancy Degenkolb, Kurt Liestenfeltz (for our aerial shots), Carissa Chappellet, and April Ping have enriched our selection with their exceptional photography.

Linda Peterson holds a special place of gardener, writer, and friend, and she contributed in each of those areas.

Indispensable in plant identification were a handful of our horticultural friends: Sarah Hammond, Sabrina and Freeland Tanner, Jonathan Plant, and Roger Warner.

Julie Bahret, Lukie Chappellet, Lygia Chappellet, Marjorie Eckels, Mary Ellis, Socorro Rodriguez, Sara Toogood, and Jayne Unander kept Molly partially sane, and assisted in the horrendous task of slide-sorting, note-taking, and computer-inputting.

We were fortunate to have a wonderful designer, Bob Aufuldish, and a great publishing team. I appreciated especially the wisdom of William LeBlond, and the suggestions and encouragement from Leslie Jonath and Sarah Putman. We would like to thank Anne Hayes for her sensitive editing and Patricia Evangelista and Michael Carabetta for their art direction.

Luanne Wells was, as usual, an invaluable support.

Special applause to Donn Chappellet, who fed us and kept us laughing.

PHOTO CREDITS

All the photographs in this book, with the exception of those listed below, were taken by Molly Chappellet.

T=top; M=middle; B=bottom; L=left; R=right

Peter Aaron/Esto
200 R, 2ND FROM T

Carissa Chappellet
91, 93 BL

Daniel D'Agostini
19, 54, 55 TL, 59 M, 60-61, 62 T, 63 BM, 70 T, 76-77, 94, 96-97, 100 ML, 101 T, 110 B, 115 T, 127 TR, 155 MR, 170, 199 BR

Nancy Degenkolb
1, 20, 21 T, 32, 37 B, 46 TL, 64 T, 122 TL, 122 TR, 123 TR

Kurt Liestenfeltz (Aerial balloon photography)
13, 41, 59, 95, 114, 188

April Ping
69; 70 R; 73 TR

Richard Tracy
7 R, 3RD FROM T; 16 B; 22 T; 24 TR; 28; 33; 45 TR; 45 TM; 45 ML; 46 TM; 52 M; 55 M; 57 B; 62 B; 63 all T photographs; 63 all M photographs; 63 BR; 65 BL; 71 T; 72; 73 B; 100 T; 100 MR; 115 ML; 123 TL; 144 TR; 180; 181 L; 181 BR; 182 BL; 198 rows 1 R, 2 L, 2 R, 3 L; 199 rows 1 L, 1 R, 2 L, 2 R, 3 R; 200 BR